STUDIES IN HIGHER EDUCATION

Edited by

Philip G. Altbach

Monan Professor of Higher Education
Lynch School of Education, Boston College

A ROUTLEDGE SERIES

STUDIES IN HIGHER EDUCATION

PHILIP G. ALTBACH, *General Editor*

ADAPTATION OF WESTERN ECONOMICS BY RUSSIAN UNIVERSITIES

INTERCULTURAL TRAVEL OF AN ACADEMIC FIELD

Tatiana Suspitsyna

Routledge
Taylor & Francis Group

LONDON AND NEW YORK

First published 2005 by Routledge

Published 2017 by Routledge
2 Park Square, Milton Park, Abingdon, Oxon OX14 4RN
711 Third Avenue, New York, NY 10017, USA

Routledge is an imprint of the Taylor & Francis Group, an informa business

First issued in paperback 2013

ISBN-13: 978-0-415-97509-4 (hbk)
ISBN-13: 978-0-415-64568-3 (pbk)

Library of Congress Card Number: 2005012434

Library of Congress Cataloging-In-Publication Data

Suspitsyna, Tatiana.
  Adaptation of Western economics by Russian universities :
  intercultural travel of an academic field / Tatiana Suspitsyna.-- 1st
  ed.
        p. cm. -- (Studies in higher education)
  Includes bibliographical references and index.
  ISBN 0-415-97509-3
  1. Economics--Study and teaching--Russia (Federation) 2.
  Cross-cultural orientation--Russia (Federation) I. Title. II. Series.

HB74.9.R8S87 2005
330'.071'147--dc22   2005012434

Taylor & Francis Group
is the Academic Division of T&F Informa plc.

Visit the Taylor & Francis Web site at
http://www.taylorandfrancis.com

and the Routledge Web site at
http://www.routledge-ny.com

For my parents

Contents

List of Figures

List of Tables

List of Appendices

Acknowledgments

This book is based on my dissertation. The travel for data collection was funded by the Spencer Foundation and the University of Michigan International Institute. The data analysis and writing were supported by the Horace H. Rackham Pre-Doctoral Fellowship at the University of Michigan.

I am profoundly grateful to the five members of my dissertation committee who contributed to my personal and professional growth and this study in various ways. Janet Lawrence has been my mentor in many intellectual and intercultural travels. Her personal and professional encouragement helped me feel at home in Ann Arbor in loco patriae. An intellectual of great academic and personal integrity, Jana Nidiffer guided me through the first years of my studies. Marvin Peterson introduced me to the organizational analysis and cultivated my interest in the political aspects of organizations. Martha Feldman opened to me the irresistible intricacies of social constructivism that I have been tirelessly exploring since. She has challenged and inspired me to learn the organization theory. Vladimir Magun has been an important link to my native academic community and I am indebted to him for his hospitality and invaluable insights about Russian academia.

I would also like to thank Tatiana Klyachko and Daria Nesterova who generously granted me their time whenever I needed help, and my colleagues at the Higher School of Economics, Moscow State University, and Ural State University for their assistance with the research. This project would have been very difficult without Jane Hassinger, who kindly offered me her office during a critical stage of my work, and Paul Lawrence, who provided me with much appreciated advice on the health aspects of dissertation writing.

I also wish to acknowledge my family, Galina Telitsyna, Anatoliy Telitsyn, and Dmitry Suspitsin, for their continuous support, and my friends Rutvica Andrijašević, William Desmond, Irina Grafova, Patricia

Mink, Patrick O'Keeffe, Vladimir Pavlovic, Ioana Szeman, and Alexandra Vrebalov for their encouragement and friendship during the years of this study.

Finally, I would like to thank Fazal Rizvi and Philip Altbach without whom this study would not have turned into a book.

Chapter One
Introduction

Long before academics began to describe the world in terms of global flows of information, expertise, capital, and technology (Appadurai, 2000; Castell, 1999, 2000), social and educational institutions of many countries benefited from the movement of ideas and practices across national boundaries. In the 19th century, Japan adapted the British model of postal service, the French model of police, and the American system of banking and art education (Westney, 1987). In the same century China introduced modern European science (Nakayama, 1984). In the post-World War II France, Renault imitated American mass production assembly techniques to become a leading automobile manufacturer in the country (Clark & Stauntan, 1990).

In a self-imposed isolation, the Soviet Union and the countries of the Soviet bloc restricted the travel of information across their national boundaries. The collapse of the Berlin Wall in 1989 and the disintegration of the Soviet Union in 1991 lifted the barriers and the flow of ideas, practices, and capital became virtually uninhibited. The newly opened Eastern and Central European nations and the former Soviet republics became eager recipients of Western investments and expertise, particularly with regard to political reforms and transition to a market economy.

This book is about the international travel of an academic field that occurred at that eventful and turbulent time.[1] Shortly after the fall of the Berlin Wall, Russian universities now open to the world began to introduce Western-style programs in economics. The country's transition to a market economy required experts in that type of economy. Trained in the Marxist-Leninist ideology that professed the imminent demise of capitalism, Soviet economists were ill equipped to produce and advance knowledge on capitalist markets—the knowledge that they had denounced as a false bourgeois science throughout their entire careers. Naturally, before the October

Revolution of 1917 Russian university curricula included disciplines on capitalist economy, which at the time was the only type of economy in existence in Europe. The Revolution changed the structure and content of higher education, demanding that academics produce practical knowledge useful for the development of the new Soviet state (David-Fox, 1997). By coercion or conviction, accepting Marxist political economy as the only correct approach to economic analysis, Russian academics of the 1920s had to reject and sever the intellectual and collaborative ties with their Western colleagues. For the next seventy years, while economics developed and generated new branches of knowledge in the West, it remained a disciplina non grata in the Soviet Union. The only source of information about it allowed to Soviet students were courses on criticism of bourgeois economic theories (Ofer & Polterovich, 2000).

The political and economic reforms of the late 1980s and early 1990s opened Russia to the Western world and caused societal changes so profound that some political scientists called them the second revolution (e.g., Hahn, 2002; Magun, 2003; McFaul, 2001). The landscape of Russian social sciences underwent transformations again. Research agendas changed priorities and foci of study. Old Soviet hierarchies of academic disciplines were rejected in favor of new curricula. Some subjects such as political economy of socialism became obsolete. Others followed the example of history of the Communist Party that metamorphosed into history of social movements and acquired new names. Still others like economics, business administration, and advertising were exported directly from abroad.

Among the transformed and exported academic subjects and disciplines, economics occupied a special place. First of all, unlike other disciplines, by virtue of its focus of study it was most intimately involved in Russia's building of a market economy. Second, appearing as the antithesis of the Marxist-Leninist economic analysis, it challenged Marxism's theoretical supremacy in the Soviet economic science. Finally, as a Western field replacing the indigenous programs in political economy, it overcame considerable local resistance and linguistic barriers. Thus, in the course of several years economics planted its roots in Russian academia. The transplantation was no small feat: Marxism in economic analysis had to be dethroned, the entire national cadre of academic economists had to be re-trained, new curricula had to be designed and implemented, economic departments had to be re-structured to accommodate new branches of knowledge, and textbooks had to be translated from English into Russian. In addition to these accomplishments in its new habitat, economics brought forth a new branch specifically for the study of post-Soviet post-socialist economy: the economics of transition.

GOALS OF THE STUDY

While there is an awareness of the fact that inclusion of Western economics in Russian higher education is vital to the preparation of experts for current reforms (Rushing, 1994; Pleskovic, Aslund, Bader & Campbell, 2000), little is known about the actual processes through which Western academic fields are introduced and adapted by post-socialist countries that intentionally isolated themselves from external influences. The few existing studies of new economics curricula in Russia are interested in reporting success stories of best educational programs rather than analyzing the process itself (see, e.g. Pleskovic et al., 2000; Shaw, Burakova & Makoukha, 2000).

At the same time, the introduction and adaptation of Western practices and institutions to non-Western contexts is not an unexplored subject. This topic has been well-developed in the studies of African institutions that copy organizational forms of their former colonial powers (Altbach, 1978, 1982, 1998; Coleman & Court, 1993; Rottenberg, 1996). It has also been studied by organization theorists. For example, in the sources mentioned earlier, Westney (1987) analyzed how Japan sent emissaries to Western Europe in the 19th century to select best organizational and institutional forms and adapted them to the military, judiciary and education systems at home. Nakayama (1984) investigated the adoption of modern European science and the rise of hygiene discourse in Japan and China in the 19th century. In a more recent study, Rottenberg (1996) examined the history of an African shipping company modeled after an American river transport company.

Furthermore, there is a growing body of literature on the adoption of Western practices in post-socialist business and industry (e.g., Camiah & Hollinshead, 2003; May, Young & Ledgerwood, 1998; Meyer & Møller, 1998; Obloj & Thomas, 1998). Perhaps, among the most relevant to this discussion are Globokar's (1997) study of French management techniques in a Slovenian plant and Stark's (2001) research on Hungarian firms. Globokar (1997) investigated how discrepancies between Western European and local beliefs about work practices led to sabotage and inefficiency. Stark (2001) demonstrated that in post-socialist settings, adoption of Western models of management requires blending them with local practices.

While these studies of adoption and adaptation of Western organizational forms and practices illuminate various aspects of the intercultural travel of ideas, there seems to be no systematic attempt to study the movement of Western academic disciplines to post-socialist higher education institutions. With the present study I attempt to begin to fill in this gap by examining how post-Soviet Russian universities have adopted and adapted the field of economics and modified their structures, practices, and organizational beliefs in the process.

My purpose in this research project is to create a comprehensive account of the adoption and adaptation of a Western academic field in a post-socialist, post-Soviet context. To meet that purpose, my inquiry is guided by the following question: How does the adaptation of Western economics by Russian universities add to the understanding of the travel of academic fields across national and cultural borders? Such a broad formulation of the research question implies that the focus of the study is complex and multifaceted, involving organizational change in universities and institutional change in the higher education system. In addition, as the studies I overviewed above suggest, the process of adaptation includes modifications in the content of the ideas and practices that are being imported. Thus, my research agenda involves three levels of investigation: disciplinary, organizational (university), and environmental. For the purpose of analysis, I divide the main question into three sub-questions according to the level of investigation: What changes occurred in the structure of Western economics as an academic field when it was adapted to the Russian context? What organizational processes occurred inside universities that adopted economics, and who were the main stakeholders of change? What actors in the external environment did the universities engage and how were they involved in the process of adapting economics? Combined, the answers to these questions will provide a comprehensive account of the intercultural travel of the Western academic field to Russian institutions of higher education.

In answering the research questions, I intend to accomplish several goals. First, I will analyze extant theoretical and empirical research on scientific fields, the imitation and adaptation of organizational forms and their institutionalization. Second, I will develop a theoretical framework that accounts for adaptation and institutionalization of academic and scientific fields in different social, economic, and political contexts. Third, I will describe the salient characteristics and recent transformations of the Russian system of higher education and provide an excursus of particularities of economic education in Russia. Fourth, I will examine changes in select Russian universities that adapted economics. Finally, I will suggest modifications to institutionalist theories and narrative approaches in organization studies.

PARAMETERS AND DEFINITIONS

A broad overarching research question such as the one guiding this inquiry requires a clear delimitation of the scope of the study. It is important, therefore, to set the parameters of this project. First, this study is not a comparative analysis of Western and Russian higher education systems. While it inevitably draws on the knowledge of the organizational structure and curriculum of Western, primarily U.S., universities, it does not set a goal or make an attempt to analyze the two systems side by side. Second, this research is not an investigation of the conceptual content of economic disciplines and the validity of their ontological assumptions and epistemological practices. I do not ask whether economics or Marxist political economy meet the criteria of good science. Instead, the analysis focuses on the beliefs and assumptions of faculty, administrators, and students about the discipline. What I do examine, however, is the structure of disciplinary content, i.e., the relations among branches and areas of economic knowledge as they are represented in university programs and curricula (e.g., Journal of Economic Literature Classification System, n.d.).

The central phenomena of the study are *economics* and *political economy*. In Western textbooks and educational programs, economics is used in at least two senses. In its narrow sense, it designates macroeconomics, microeconomics and econometrics (cf. Ofer & Polterovich, 2000). In its broader sense, it refers to the entire field of economics that, in addition to general macro and microeconomic theories, includes a wide range of specialized areas of study, e.g., industrial organizations, labor economics, public finance, transitional economics, etc. (Journal of Economic Literature Classification System, n.d.). Similarly, political economy, most often defined as Marxist political economy, refers to Marx's economic theory and to a set of disciplines derived from Marx's intellectual heritage, e.g., Marxist philosophy and historical materialism in addition to Marxist political economy (cf. Ofer & Polterovich, 2000). As the purpose of this project is to examine an academic field rather than individual academic subjects, unless specified otherwise, I use economics and political economy synecdochically, i.e. as representations of their entire fields. Furthermore, to stress the foreign origins of the discipline and contrast them to the Soviet academic tradition, I give economics designations "Western" and "mainstream."

Another necessary clarification concerns the use of the term *higher education institution* and *innovation*. Since the study draws on institutionalist theoretical approaches, it is important to differentiate between institution as a social practice (e.g., the institution of marriage) and institution as an organization (e.g., a university). To avoid the conflation of the two, wherever possible I provide the context to make the meaning of the term unambiguous. Although the term *innovation* is rather straightforward, meaning introduction of something new, its use has acquired considerable theoretical baggage. Organization studies and higher education literature are replete with models and definitions of innovation (e.g., Damanpour, 1987, 1990; Fullan, 1991; Hage & Aiken, 1970; Harvey & Mills, 1970; Huberman & Miles, 1984; King, 1990; Nord & Tucker, 1987; Rogers, 1983; Zaltman, Duncan & Holbek, 1973). However, in this study, I employ the term in a generic sense, referring to none of the existing innovation theories, unless specified otherwise.

Similarly, I use the terms *adoption* and *adaptation* in their dictionary meanings. By *adoption* I understand the process of formally accepting ideas, structures, or practices and putting them into effect, while *adaptation* is defined as the process of modifying ideas, structures, and practices to make them fit to particular contexts.

Finally, I believe a note on my audience and my identity as a researcher is appropriate in this international study. The book is written with two audiences in mind: English-speaking Western and English-speaking Russian academics and supporters of educational reforms. The two audiences adhere to their own conventions of academic writing, which overlap but do not coincide. For example, the use of the first person narrative is permitted in Western academic texts but frowned upon in Russian scholarly publications. As a Russian scholar trained at an American university, I adhere to both styles. However, since this research project was conducted as part of my doctoral studies in the U.S., in this book I adopt the first person narrative.

SIGNIFICANCE OF THE STUDY

This study has theoretical, empirical, and practical significance. The project makes at least three theoretical contributions. First, the study's theoretical framework provides a conceptual apparatus for future research on the international and intercultural exchange of scholarship and institutional forms. Second, combining institutionalism in organization studies with social studies of science, the study offers a synthesis of two philosophically close strands of theories. Third, drawing on the insights from translation and narrative analysis, it contributes to the development of institutional theories by charting directions for research that includes linguistic analyses.

The study's empirical value is at least two-fold. First, it adds to higher education and organization studies literature on international exchange, adoption and adaptation of academic ideas and practices. Second, employing cases together with narrative analyses in its research design, the study creates a methodological strategy for examining both material and symbolic changes in organizations.

The practical significance of this research project consists of its implications for Russian and Western organizations and higher education institutions engaged in the research and support of the intercultural transfer and development of new disciplines. First, the study outlines the general mechanisms through which universities participating in the global exchange of ideas adopt and adapt academic disciplines, structures, and practices borrowed from other national and cultural contexts. Second, it uncovers peculiarities of adapting Western academic fields in post-Soviet post-socialist university contexts, revealing the sources of faculty resistance and strategies for change. Finally, since by virtue of providing knowledge for current market reforms, economics is implicated in Russia's project of national revival, the study of the discipline offers valuable insights about the nexus among academic developments, Soviet cultural traditions, and larger political processes in that country.

ORGANIZATION OF THE BOOK

The book is organized in eight chapters. Following the first introductory chapter, Chapter Two outlines the theoretical framework of the study. Chapter Three explicates the research design and data collection methods as well as measures enhancing the quality of data analysis. Chapter Four sets the background of the study by providing an overview of Russian higher education and highlighting major issues facing Russian academic economists, and introduces the first case of a select Russian university that adapted economics. Chapters Five and Six present the second and the third university cases in the book. Chapter Seven offers an integrative analysis of the three cases and suggests implications for the intercultural travel of academic fields. Finally, Chapter Eight draws conclusions and proposes directions for further research.

Chapter Two
Conceptualizing Travel of Academic Fields: A Theoretical Framework

When Russian academics began to introduce economics in the late 1980s and early 1990s, it had changed significantly from what it was seventy years before, when Russian and Western economic sciences parted ways after the October Revolution. The neoclassical and institutionalist economic theories of the 1920s and 1930s, the Keynesianism of the decades following World War II, and the neo-conservatism of the 1970s and 1980s expanded the theoretical boundaries of the discipline and contributed to the foundation and development of various branches of economic knowledge (Fusfeld, 1999). By the time the Berlin Wall fell in 1989, economics represented a mature disciplinary tree with branches and limbs covering various areas of economic life. The transplantation of the discipline from its native organizational habitat into the Russian soil involved modifications both in the disciplinary tree and in the receiving universities.

In order to examine these modifications, I adopt a double lens of two theoretical approaches. The first is known under the umbrella term of social studies of science. I employ it to define the structure and boundaries of economics as a scientific field and explain its place in larger social, political, and economic networks. Represented by institutionalism in organization studies, the second approach provides me with a framework for analyzing adaptation processes and organizational changes that occurred in Russian universities as they introduced economics.

CONCEPTUALIZATIONS OF SCIENCES AND SCIENTIFIC FIELDS

Classical sociology of science examines scientific fields and disciplines for their compliance with the criteria of rigorous scholarship, pursuit of scientific truth, and their distance from politics (Merton, 1957, 1978). Best expressed in the works of Robert Merton, it stresses the role of scholarly norms and culture (or ethos, in Merton's terminology) in the development of science as an institution. Although classical sociologists of science acknowledge the influence of social, political, and economic factors on the development of science, the non-academic environment is regarded with suspicion as a potential source of contamination with non-scientific concerns and agendas.

A Mertonian institutional analysis of science informed the thinking behind a number of studies of academic communities in the 1970s and 1980s. Perhaps, the most well-known of them is Diane Crane's *Invisible Colleges* (1972). Crane studied the development of two academic fields, rural sociology and a research area in algebra. She noticed that scientific growth is not only a cognitive process but also a social one and that the development of fields of study occurs faster when there is more interaction among scholars. Crane observed that often valuable exchanges and diffusion of ideas occurred through "invisible colleges": informal scholarly communications via personal correspondence and conversations, and interactions between professors and graduate students.

In the decades following the publication of Crane's book, more social scientists took upon themselves the task of describing science from the institutional perspective. Robin Clarke (1985) expanded on Crane's metaphor of invisible colleges, by introducing the notions of visible (e.g., national and international scholarly associations) and political colleges (e.g., science advisory systems that work with national governments and international organizations) (Clarke, 1985). Tony Becher modified Crane's ideas about interpersonal scholarly networks as guardians of paradigms by adding to them the element of specialized research interests developed elsewhere (c.f. Mulkay, 1977). In his quasi-ethnographic work on "academic tribes and territories," Becher (1987, 1989) described a diverse panorama of disciplinary groups, professional norms, and methodological practices, suggesting that scholarly communities may be part of "social circles" that extend into the world outside of the academy.

Although for scholars like Crane, Clarke, and Becher the development of scientific disciplines has both cognitive and social aspects, the social component refers mostly to interactions among academics and not to the production of knowledge itself. From their perspective, the scientific enterprise consists mostly of and for scholars, who interact with the outside world (e.g., through Clark's political colleges or Becher's social circles) but should never be invested in its interests or allow it to participate in the actual pursuit of scientific truth. In other words, whereas science interacts with other social institutions and organizations, it keeps its core function and raison d'être—the production of knowledge—uninfluenced by the social, political, and economic forces in the environment.

Coming from diverse disciplinary backgrounds, critics of the Mertonian view of science question its disengagement from political interests and social values. For instance, Bourdieu (1980, 1991) asserts that science is a cultural production reflecting power relations among social institutions and actors: "[t]he structure of the scientific field is defined, at every moment, by the state of the relations of power among the protagonists in the struggle . . . It is this structure that assigns to each scientist his or her strategies and scientific stances, and the objective chances for their success, depending on the position he/she occupies in it" (Bourdieu, 1991, p. 9). Feminists also note the political implications of science, particularly with regard to its gender bias and exclusion of women (e.g., Haraway, 1997; Harding, 1991; Keller, 1988; Schiebinger, 1989; Sørensen, 1992), while discourse analysts, anthropologists, and students of culture point at the ways science exerts political influence on government policies and the public through the mystification of scientific enterprise and claims of truth (e.g., Ashmore, Myers, & Potter, 1995; Gregory & Miller, 1998; LaFollette, 1990;Toumey, 1996).

What unites most of these critics of the Mertonian sociology of science is the shift in the focus of study from the institution of science to the production of knowledge. Even more importantly, this shift coincides with the paradigmatic change from positivism to social constructivism with its relativist epistemology and deep suspicion of claims at objectivity, autonomy, and truth. For instance, studies of laboratory work demonstrate that scientists do not describe nature through their research, as the positivists would have it, but abstract it, reproduce it in their labs for experimental manipulation and then re-construct it in the form of a scientific fact (Gaudillière & Löwy, 1998, Latour & Woolgar, 1979; Latour, 1999; Lynch, 1985; Knorr-Cetina, 1992, 1995, 1999). Furthermore, the production of scientific facts from germs (Latour, 1984; 1999) to steppes (Williams, 2000) to quarks (Pickering, 1995) and quaternions (Pickering & Stephanides, 1992) involves a considerable amount of negotiation among researchers, scholarly communities, and social actors. Since research often requires a dependence on high technology industry, science can no longer be described as autonomous (Cutcliffe, 2000; Latour, 1996) and the boundaries of science become hard to delineate (Gieryn, 1995, 1999; Latour, 1987; Lenoir, 1993, 1997; Nowotny, Scott, & Gibbons, 2001; Taylor, 1996).

Known under the umbrella term of social studies of science, these multidisciplinary investigations of the production of knowledge cast new light on the relationship between science and its social, political, and economic environments. For social constructivists, external influences on the production of scientific facts is not necessarily a threat to research, but a natural part of it. Research agendas are often dictated by industry; governments shape research priorities through policy-making, banning some types of research and endorsing others; the public intervenes in the development of scientific fields on ethical or religious grounds; and finally, increasingly sophisticated technologies and tools become as indispensable to knowledge production as scientists themselves.

Bruno Latour (1999) captures the interconnectedness of social and scholarly spheres in his conceptualization of the scientific field. In contrast to the Mertonian view of science, where the conceptual core is protected from the external environment, Latour (1999) treats core disciplinary knowledge as a flow of ideas that is sustained by networks of people, organizations, and artifacts. The entire scientific field is represented as five interactive networks: the conceptual core of the science; academic institutions and communities; allies in political, social and economic spheres; public opinion; and the instrumental and methodological apparatus that the field employs to study phenomena (tools, formulae, artifacts, etc.) (Latour, 1999).

Latour envisions these networks as blood flows to the heart of science—its conceptual core. Academics and their invisible colleges guard the criteria of scholarship and decide whether newly produced knowledge can be counted as scientific facts. Politicians, governments, industrialists, and entrepreneurs develop their own interests in scientific research and sponsor science for those reasons. Companies organize research labs and manufacture their own state of the art laboratory equipment, further blurring the boundaries between science and industry. In an era of mass communication, along with the increasing demands for ecological and ethical accountability of science, the public may support one type of research and seek to ban another. Finally, scientific artifacts, specimen, formulae, and measurements represent a non-human participant of scientific networks. Invented or, as Latour (1999) puts it, fabricated by scientists, these artifacts, specimen, and formulae acquire a life independent of their creators and continue their existence in museums, libraries, scholarly publications, etc.

While this model is useful as a framework for conceptualizing economics in this study, it requires a shift in emphasis. One limitation of Latour's model is that as a definition of the scientific field, it is excessively externalist, i.e. it overemphasizes the role of the external nonacademic environment in the production of knowledge. Although the role of internal disciplinary forces such as norms and rules of scholarship are implied in his conceptualization of academic communities, for the purposes of this particular study they will be given greater prominence in the analysis. The focus on professional norms will be especially useful in the analyses of Russian universities' decisions about the appropriateness of Western knowledge and academic practices for their institutions. Academics and administrators may have different opinions about what is considered legitimate and appropriate, and the same innovation may meet scholarly criteria but contradict the existing organizational norms.

A Latourian model of economics helps one comprehend changes within the academic field as it has been adapted to new cultural and institutional settings. Entering the Russian academic space, Western economics persuaded local academics of its legitimacy, circumvented the bureaucracy of the Ministry of Education, found its place in the existing education system, attracted supporters inside and outside of academe, and became part of the nation's project of creating a capitalist market through theory-building and policy making. Thus, economics as a social science was developed through input from academics and academic institutions, stakeholders in the government, economic, political and social spheres, and last but not least, sustained by the market as an object of study. Figure 2.1 shows a graphic representation of the networks of economics as an academic field adapted from Latour's (1999) model of a scientific field.

The social studies of science conceptualization of economics as dynamic networks implies that as one part of those interconnected networks, universities interact continuously with the external environment. From the organizational theory perspective, the universities act as open systems, i.e., as systems that are "capable of self-maintenance on the basis of a throughput of resources from the environment" (Scott, 1998, p. 89). Conceptualizing organizations as open systems, institutionalist theories explain how organizations copy ideas and practices from one another and become alike. Applied to the case of economics, the institutionalist theories help one understand how and why Russian universities copied economics from Western universities and what happened to the innovation and its adopters in the process.

INSTITUTIONALIST APPROACHES TO THE STUDY OF ORGANIZATIONS

Beginning with Talcott Parsons (1937), institutional analyses of organizations developed in response to rational choice theories (see, for example, scientific management of Frederick Taylor [1911]). Institutionalists like

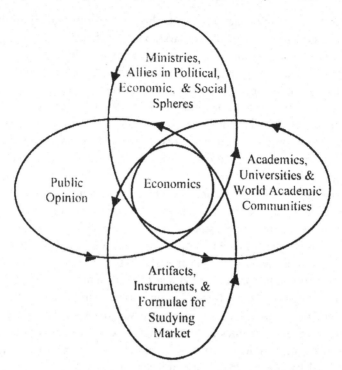

Figure 2.1. Networks of Economics as an Academic Field

Parsons and Selznick (1949) following him, believed that individuals and organizations follow the logic of appropriateness rather than the logic of consequentiality (March & Olsen, 1989), i.e. they choose a course of action that is most appropriate for preserving conformity in a given situation rather than calculate maximally beneficial outcomes.

In the field of higher education, Selznick's analysis was furthered by Burton Clark (1956) who studied the difficulties of adult education programs in Los Angeles and Brint and Karabel (1991) who studied community colleges. Like Selznick, Clark (1956) examined the history of the organization under study, its initial mission and goals, and like Selznick, he tied the change in the goals, or goal displacement, to the pressures to acquire more legitimacy with external actors. Although chronologically Brint and Karabel's work (1991) belongs to the period of new institutionalism, intellectually it continues Selznick's tradition with its focus on organizational change and goal displacement resulting from co-optation of external elements.

In the mid-sixties, Selznick's institutionalism underwent several modifications, influenced by two ground breaking works: Berger and Luckmann's (1966) book on the social construction of reality and Garfinkel's ethnomethodology (1967) (DiMaggio & Powell, 1991a). An important part of Berger and Luckmann's conceptualization of institutionalization is so-called habitualized actions which they define as a pattern of repeated actions whose meanings become routinized and taken for granted as part of the general stock of knowledge (Berger & Luckmann, 1966, p. 53–54). Like Berger and Luckmann, albeit by a different methodological route, Garfinkel (1967) also discovered the importance of taken-for-granted knowledge that actors use to understand and reproduce social institutions around them. Thus, for Berger and Luckmann, and for Garfinkel, institutional power is exerted in a subtler way than the old institutionalism would have it: institutions structure individuals' actions not so much by imposing moral norms but by making them internalized as routine knowledge.

The books by Berger and Luckman, and Garfinkel facilitated a transition from the old institutionalism of Parsons and Selznick to new institutionalism whose origins are associated primarily with the works of John Meyer (DiMaggio & Powell, 1991a). This transition initiated several shifts in foci of study and interpretation: from organizational change to organizational stability; from direct and actual interactions among members of organizational fields to symbolic and virtual connections among members of organizational fields (Czarniawska, 2004)[1]; from moral norms to "deeply ingrained" understandings of social reality (Meyer & Rowan, 1991, p. 24)[2].

With institutionalization defined as "the processes by which social processes, obligations, or actualities come to take on a rule-like status in social thought and action" (Meyer & Rowan, 1991, p. 22), the institutional model of education is founded on two premises. First, the structures of educational organizations reflect institutionalized rules and norms about education in the environment (Meyer, Scott & Deal, 1981). This means that schools reflect societal beliefs about legitimate educational organizations: schools are accredited and classified by type and student age; students are grouped by age and occasionally by ability. For the most part, curricula consist of a widely accepted range of topics, school teachers are licensed, and college faculty have terminal degrees. Furthermore, because the source of legitimacy for schools is located with environmental social and authority systems rather than the market, education as an institution is closely connected to social and political institutions (Meyer, 1992a). Second, instructional activity is decoupled from organizational structures:

although educational organizations have administrators and managers, typically, they cannot control what is going on in the classroom (Meyer, Scott & Deal, 1981). Hence the paradox: on the one hand, instruction needs to be controlled to ensure quality; on the other hand, instruction should not be controlled lest control infringe on professors' academic freedom (Meyer & Rowan, 1991).[3]

Schools, colleges, and universities as organizations belong to organizational fields. With their vastly stretched boundaries, organizational fields include "organizations that, in the aggregate, constitute a recognized area of institutional life: key suppliers, resource and product consumers, regulatory agencies, and other organizations that produce similar services or products" (DiMaggio and Powell, 1991b, pp. 64–65). Therefore, the organizational field of education consists of not only schools, colleges, and universities, but also their boards, legislatures, parent and community groups and other structures that express "the formal relations of authority that manage education within a broader institutional context of customs, rules, understandings, taken-for-granted practices, and so on" (Meyer, 1992d, p. 235). In sum, the boundaries of the institution of education reach far beyond the physical places of learning.

The institutional context of education, or more precisely, its institutional environment is the source of legitimacy for schools, colleges, and universities. They survive by becoming more alike, or isomorphing, with their institutional environment even at the expense of efficiency (Meyer & Rowan, 1991; Meyer & Zucker, 1989).[4] The isomorphic pressures may come from different sources. For instance, schools may be forced to introduce new elements by the power of the law or public opinion; they may want to improve their performance by adopting innovations that have proven to be successful elsewhere; or they may be compelled to bring in new practices to preserve their place in the professional field. In DiMaggio and Powell's typology (1991b), these examples illustrate coersive, mimetic, and normative isomorphism, respectively. Coersive isomorphic change occurs under external pressure from other organizations and from the cultural expectations of society at large. Mimetic isomorphism consists of imitation of successful organizations under conditions of uncertainty and ambiguity, whereas the source of normative isomorphism is professionalization (DiMaggio & Powell, 1991b).

The notion of isomorphism is key to the new institutionalist conceptualizations of change and innovation. Broadly defined as the introduction of environmental elements in organizations, innovation is an organizational mechanism for adjusting to environments. Unlike innovation models based on rational-choice theories (e.g. Rogers, 1983; Rogers & Shoemaker, 1971), new institutionalism suggests that innovation as organizational action follows the logic of appropriateness (March & Olsen, 1989) and that even if innovations are initially introduced to improve efficiency, they reach a threshold beyond which they no longer improve efficiency but serve to maintain legitimacy (Meyer & Rowan, 1991, 1992). Furthermore, the adoption of innovations is guided by the myths of rationality. For instance, schools introducing innovations must first establish the rationality of their decision and thus ensure the legitimacy of their action by justifying innovations scientifically, publicizing their successful adoption, and by couching their desire to adopt in moral reformist terms (Meyer, 1992c).

In addition to external normative forces, organizational decisions to introduce innovations are also influenced by the interior cognitive order that shapes actors' understanding of reality (Friedland & Alford, 1991). Since institutions are "simultaneously material and ideal, systems of signs and symbols, rational and transrational" (Friedland & Alford; 1991, p. 243), innovation involves both material and symbolic change. Because the shifts in the objective relations and symbolic meanings reflect shifts in power, institutionalist analyses of organizational innovations also involve a political analysis (DiMaggio, 1988; Friedland & Alford, 1991).

The insistent emphasis of new institutionalism on stability and the preclusion of change through imitation and diffusion attracted considerable criticism on the part of organizational theorists. An international group of scholars from the U.S. and Scandinavian countries addressed this criticism by elaborating some new institutionalist propositions in a series of works that together came to be known as Scandinavian institutionalism. A result of intellectual exchanges initiated by March and Meyer in the U.S. and Olsen and Brunsson in Europe, Scandinavian institutionalism assumes that organizational norms include both stability and change and that the logic of appropriateness complements the logic of consequentiality (Czarniawska & Sevón, 1996).

One of the concepts revised in this cross-disciplinary inquiry is diffusion. Noting that diffusion involves more than dissemination, Scandinavian institutionalists follow Callon and Latour (1981) in proposing to replace the term with *translation*. Translation involves both the movement and change of linguistic and material objects during diffusion (Callon & Latour, 1981) and thus better reflects adoption and diffusion of innovations across institutional and national boundaries. As Czarniawska and Joerges (1996) explain, when institutions and organizations move, or "travel," from one cultural context to another, they are not simply imitated and replicated anew. Rather, they are modified or "translated" by the receiving environment so that they are understood and accepted by organizational members and stakeholders, supporters in the political, economic, and social spheres, and by the public in general. Thus, imitation is a "process in which something is created and transformed by chains of translators" (Sevón, 1996, p. 51) and it involves change along with copying.

The linguistic properties of translation of organizational forms and ideas open up new possibilities for analyzing organizational narratives of innovation and change. For example, Sahlin-Andersson and Sevón (2003) re-conceptualized translation as an editing process and examined organizational stories of innovation for editing rules. They discovered three rules: organizations necessarily change the temporal and spatial contexts of the prototype to fit it into their own structure and culture; organizations create meta-narratives about the prototype in order for it to be accepted; and finally, accounts of adoption follow the plot of rational change and improvement (Sahlin-Andersson & Sevón, 2003). Drawing on cultural studies, Czarniawska (1997) developed a narrative approach to the study of organizational identity. With the metaphor of the world-as-text at the center of her inquiry, she is interested in the construction of stories that govern the lives of individuals and the society as a whole (Czarniawska, 1997). Other scholars of organizational narratives examined how stories established a framework within which organizational members understood the meaning of change (Boje, 1991) and how they served to reinforce organizational values and identities (Feldman and Sköldberg, 2002).

BRINGING SOCIAL STUDIES OF SCIENCE AND INSTITUTIONALISM TOGETHER

Combining concepts from social studies of science and institutionalism enhances the analytic capacity of this study by creating a lens for analyzing both the traveling discipline and the hosting educational organization. Institutionalism shapes the investigation of rationalization and changes in organizational time and space in the universities that adapted economics. Social studies of science frame the inquiry into the components of economics as a scientific field: the discipline itself; the phenomena it studies in the real world; universities and academic communities; actors in the government, political, social, and economic spheres; and public opinion.

Applied to the case of economics in Russia, the combined approach establishes underlying premises of the study. First, economics as an academic and scientific field presents an interconnected network of ideas (conceptual core), people and organizations (faculty, students, universities, etc.), allies in the political, economic, and social spheres (granting agencies, ministries, etc.), the public (parents, communities with vested interests in economic education), and artifacts (economic theories, surveys, reports, methodological instruments, etc.). Second, universities under study are educational organizations that are structured by and enact the rules of the social institution of education. Third, the process of adaptation and diffusion of economics in the universities under study is understood as an intercultural translation of an innovation. Fourth, the translation of economics in the Russian context involves material and symbolic change, i.e. change in universities' organizational structures and practices as well as in the understanding of social reality by their administrators, faculty, and students. Finally, the outcome of the translation of economics is institutionalization of the discipline in Russian higher education, i.e. economics becomes a habitual organized academic practice.

Examining economics as a scientific field and investigating changes in Russian universities, I employ the two theoretical approaches to varying degrees and in various combinations. On the one hand, the discussion of the market as a phenomenon studied by economics is informed mostly by Latour's (1999) conceptualizations of the non-human world of science. On the other hand, the analysis of the linguistic and structural translations of economic fields and branches in Russian universities is based on the concept of translation developed by Scandinavian institutionalists, who, in turn, borrowed it from Latour and his colleagues. The examination of change processes in the universities and academic communities draws primarily on institutionalist interpretations of isomorphism and legitimacy of organizations in organizational fields. The idea of legitimacy is also central to the discussion of select components in the networks comprising economics as a scientific field, specifically, supporters in non-academic spheres and public opinion.

Chapter Three
Research Design and Methods

This explanatory study of the adaptation of Western economics in Russia includes analyses of ideas, actors, processes, and artifacts that are involved in material and symbolic changes in Russian universities. Previous research on change in organizations in general and higher education organizations in particular suggest that cases (Clark, 1956; Epper, 1997; Hammond, 1984; Hartley, 1994; Selznick, 1949; Stensaker & Norgard, 2001; Van Loon, 2001) and narrative analytical approaches (Clark, 1972; Czarniawska, 1997; Gabriel, 1998, 2000; Morril, Yalda, Adelman, Musheno, & Bejarano, 2000) are effective tools for conducting such studies. In this investigation I employ both methods complementarily. The cases reflect the accounts of adaptation presented in official university publications, while the narrative analysis adds the perspectives of individuals who participated in this change process to the cases.

CASES, STORIES, AND ENTHYMEMES

I use a multiple-case research design with the idea that all cases in the study illustrate the same outcome, i.e., all cases follow the logic of literal replication (Yin, 1989). Consisting of three cases, this research has a greater analytic generalizability (Yin, 1989), which enhances the validity of theoretical conclusions about the overall process of intercultural travel of academic fields. Furthermore, a case study allows me to create a comprehensive portrait of actors, objects, events, and contexts related to the adaptation of economics in Russia, by examining phenomena and processes in their natural settings without controlling or intervening in the situation (Bensabat, Goldstein & Mead, 1987; Stake, 1995). With a change process as the unit of analysis, the cases focus on how universities introduced and adapted economics, modifying their structure in the process.

Although the cases draw both on facts and perceptions to create a picture of organizational change, they may not be adept at analyzing finer points of actors' perceptions, beliefs, and assumptions that underlie organizational action and that are expressed in organizational stories. The study of organizational stories is important because it illuminates tacit rules, beliefs and taken-for-granted knowledge about reality that organizational members use to make sense of the every-day world around them (Weick, 1995; Boje, 1991). Furthermore, scholars point out that as transmitters of rules, organizational stories shape actors' behavior by defining appropriate interpretations and courses of action. This ability of stories to influence organizational members' behavior through assumptions and premises prompted Perrow (1986) to call them 'premise controls' and classify them in importance after direct supervision and supervision through written documents. Finally, organizational stories serve to reinforce organizational values and identities (Czarniawska, 1997; Feldman & Sköldberg, 2002). Given the emphasis of institutionalist theories on organizational rules and tacit knowledge of routines, an analysis of organizational stories promises useful insights. Thus, in addition to the cases, I use a narrative analytical approach in this study. Specifically, I employ an approach known as a rhetorical analysis of organizational stories.

While case study as a research design and method has been established for at least half a century, rhetorical analysis is relatively new in organization studies (e.g., Roberts, 1999; Watson, 1995) and social studies of science (e.g., Gibson, 2003). The method consists of uncovering implicit meanings in a story, by examining each sentence for an incomplete syllogism (enthymeme) and applying the rules of classical logic to infer its missing premises (Feldman, 2004; Feldman and Sköldberg, 2002). Central to the method, the concept of enthymeme has its origins in Aristotelian rhetoric. According to Aristotle (1953, p. 80), an enthymeme is a short syllogism, "out of which that which is supposed to be necessarily understood by the hearer is left as superfluous; to avoid prolixity" and which "neither concludes out of everything nor out of remote principles" (p. 139). In other words, an enthymeme is an incomplete syllogism, or logical inference, where one part is missing and the conclusion is probable rather than necessary (Aristotle, 1995). For example, the argument "Some faculty were dissatisfied with the level of instruction at the old universities, therefore they founded a new university" (adapted from an interview) is an example of an enthymeme consisting of two parts: the minor premise "some faculty were dissatisfied with the level of instruction at the old universities" and the conclusion "therefore they founded a new university." In the context of the story, the listener or reader of this argument has to provide the major premise on her own, inferring that "old universities have a low level of instruction." Since the inference makes sense in the given situation, it is assumed to be logical and true.

Whereas listeners and readers do not habitually analyze the assumptions underlying what they hear and read, researchers, interested in uncovering the implicit text of the story, do. Reconstructing the assumed major premise turns the initial enthymeme into a complete syllogism: (a) the reconstructed major premise "old universities have a low level of instruction;" (b) the minor premise "some faculty were dissatisfied with the level of instruction at the old universities;" and (c) the conclusion "therefore they founded a new university." A closer examination of the reconstructed enthymeme reveals that the syllogism is flawed: although the conclusion is probable, it is not necessarily true, that is, it is not logically binding. For example, improving the level of instruction at the old universities is as plausible a conclusion as founding a new university; the old universities having an unreachably high level of instruction is as likely a major premise as their having an unsatisfactorily low level of instruction.

Thus, with one of its premises or conclusion missing, the enthymeme omits the common or controversial information and engages the audience in the co-construction of meaning, leading them to a desired understanding. For this quality, the enthymeme was regarded by Aristotle (1953) as one of the most effective methods of persuasion. In the text, the enthymeme is often supported by other rhetorical figures such as opposition, an exemplar (an example that illustrates the argument), or a sign (an indication of something else that serves to reinforce the argument).

In this study, I construct the cases primarily on the basis of information from university publications, websites, academic plans, and syllabi. In other words, the cases draw on the officially accepted and approved texts. By contrast, for the rhetorical analysis I use personal narratives of individuals engaged in the process of adapting economics. Whereas the cases are focused on the processes and events leading to the introduction and adaptation of the new discipline, the rhetorical analysis reveals the tacit and taken for granted knowledge and assumptions governing actors' behavior in these processes and events. Figure 3.1 offers a graphic representation of the relationship between the case method and narrative analyses employed in this study.

The rhetorical analysis enriches the case study at least in three ways. First, it uncovers the implicit assumptions about academic work that organizational members enact in their storytelling as opposed to the values that

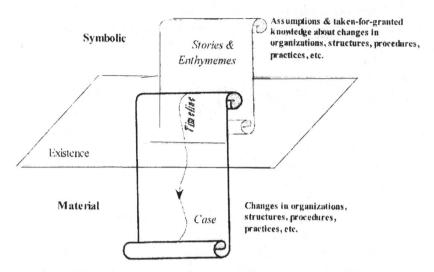

Figure 3.1. The Use of Case and Narrative Analyses in the Study

are officially propagated by the administration. In the case of economics in Russian universities, it helps explain the incongruence between the universities' declarations about internationalizing their curricula and the rejection of Western academic practices by some faculty. Second, the rhetorical analysis illuminates how organizational stories communicate and reinforce institutional identities, particularly in relation to organizational pasts. Given the major ideological shifts within Russian universities that adopted and adapted economics, institutional identities came to include a mix of both educational systems and worldviews, Soviet and Western, rather than a new homogeneously Western worldview (cf. Bartunek, 1984). Third, the rhetorical analysis of organizational stories shows how organizational members' tacit understandings and assumptions worked as premise controls (Perrow, 1986), prescribing a course of action in various situations. In Russian universities, most faculty and administrators formed a set of assumptions about designing programs and courses in economics that became blueprints for future curricular development.

RESEARCH SITES

My research sites are Moscow State University (MSU), the Higher School of Economics (HSE), and Ural State University (USU). In selecting these sites, I followed several criteria. First, the selected universities had to be ranked highly by their peers and potentially serve as models for imitation to other higher education institutions in the country. Second, the sites had to be accessible to me as a researcher. Understanding access as a relational process developing over time (Feldman, Bell, & Berger, 2003, p. vii), I traveled regularly to Russia from 1998 to 2003 first to establish and then to cultivate relations with faculty and administrators in several universities. In 2000–2002, I participated in a Ford Foundation sponsored project on economics education in Russia, which strengthened my ties to the local communities of economists and helped me earn their trust and respect. Several academics expressed enthusiastic interest in my research and offered assistance with data collection. This overall supportive attitude created a unique opportunity to access people and materials that are not readily available to researchers, especially to those traveling from abroad.

Finally, my third criterion of site selection was based on the principle of "fill[ing] theoretical categories and provid[ing] examples of polar types" (Eisenhardt, 1989, p. 537). Higher education literature describes organizational and curricular change in higher education as involving three constituent groups: students (e.g., Brooker & Macdonald, 1999; Stark & Letucca, 1997), faculty (e.g., Hickson, 2000; Stark & Letucca, 1997), and administrators (e.g., Hickson, 2000; Wolverton, 1998). In my conversations with Russian academics during the preliminary phase of the study, it emerged that MSU, HSE, and USU represented three distinct cases where the change toward Western economic approaches was initiated by administrators, faculty, and students, respectively. The purposeful selection of diverse organizational cases had a potential for extending the theory (Eisenhardt, 1989) and it is for this reason that MSU, HSE, and USU were selected as appropriate research sites.

All three institutions are public. Among the three, the Higher School of Economics is the youngest university—it was opened in the wake of economic reforms in the early 1990s. Moscow State University is the oldest university in the country and it is traditionally considered the most prestigious. Ural State University is the largest and the oldest university in the industrial Ural Region, a thousand miles from Moscow. Many faculty members in HSE and USU are graduates of MSU. All three schools are ranked highly by their peers for the quality of their faculty and programs in economics. Table 3.1 summarizes the main features of the three universities.

Table 3.1. Main Characteristics of the Selected Research Sites

University Characteristic	Moscow State University	Higher School of Economics	Ural State University
Type of Control	Public/State	Public/State	Public/State
Location	Moscow	Moscow	Ekaterinburg
Year of Foundation	1755	1992	1920
Total Student Enrollment	45,000	7,400	6,500
Student Enrollment in Economic Programs	3,000	1,800	500

DATA COLLECTION

The planning and data collection consisted of three phases. The first, preliminary phase was completed in 2000 and 2001 and consisted mostly of 'orientation' conversations and visits that served to gain general ideas about research sites and potential respondents as well as questions for interview protocols for the next stages of my project (Hartley, 1994).

Most of the data were collected in Phase 2 in July-August of 2002, when I conducted interviews and collected documents for analysis. Thirty-six semi-structured hour-long interviews were conducted across three universities. The selection of subjects was conducted in two steps. The names of two-thirds of the respondents were identified through preliminary examination of university websites and conversations with faculty and graduates during Phase 1. This target group of respondents included faculty members, graduates, and administrators who were actively involved in structural and curricular changes at their institutions. Second, the remaining respondents were identified on a recommendation basis, that is, through the interviews with the target group subjects. The respondents were recommended as persons knowledgeable about the introduction of economics in Russian universities.

The interviews were structured around several areas: introduction of economics in the local curriculum; sources of influence on and support of the new curricular model; ratios of Russian and Western components of economics courses and programs; and scholarly collaboration with Western and Russian scholars. Two additional questions asked for respondents' personal data and inquired about other individuals who might be included in the study. Before the data collection in Russia, I piloted the interview protocol with three Russian doctoral students in economics at a large Midwestern university and made modifications. The original protocol is attached in Appendix A.

Collecting data through interviews presented an unexpected problem with respondents' reactions to the consent form. The research design, interview protocol, and consent form were approved by my university's Institutional Review Board (IRB) with the caveat that requested that respondents must consent to participation in writing. Although I explained that the consent form served to protect the rights of respondents, four of the approached subjects adamantly refused to sign the form, but agreed to be interviewed. In each of the four cases, I politely turned down the offer to proceed with the interview and terminated the session. The respondents' refusal to sign the form was emotional (in one instance, the subject threw the forms on the floor). As became clear from their remarks, the refusers felt that by not putting their name at the end of the document they safeguarded their anonymity, and vice versa, by signing a paper, especially prepared by a foreign organization, they were putting themselves at risk of being penalized, should their participation in foreign research be deemed undesirable. From the thirty-six respondents who did sign the consent forms, twenty-five agreed to be recorded on an audiotape, while eleven allowed me to take written notes only.

The majority of the recorded respondents were faculty members with a full-time appointment at their universities. All audio-taped administrators in the study had teaching responsibilities in their departments. The respondent groups at Moscow State and the Higher School of Economics consisted of faculty and administrators: eight faculty and six administrators at MSU and six faculty and three administrators at HSU. Many of these respondents were themselves graduates of MSU or HSE. In addition to eight faculty members and three administrators, respondents at Ural State University included two USU graduates who did not have a full-time appointment at that university. However, both of them taught there at different times[1]. All of the respondents were either directly involved in the introduction and adaptation of economics in their institutions or, in the case of junior faculty members, they experienced them as students. The composition of samples on the three campuses is a limitation of this study: presumably, individuals who did not witness or were not involved in the development of economics in Russia would have different responses to interview questions. The fact that respondents on each of the three campuses had similar organizational stories to share may testify both to the pervasiveness and power of organizational stories and to the limitation of samples.

Whereas interviews present a perceptual picture of change, document analysis offers factual support of personal recollections and reconstructions of experiences. In the context of this study, by *factual* I understand recorded in official documents and publications. To describe the changes in economics in

Russian universities, I utilized several types of documents: academic plans (*uchebnii plan*) in economics departments; course syllabi; so-called state Standards of Higher Education—legal documents prescribing university curricula issued by the Ministry of Education; minutes of the academic council meetings; university publications and newsletters, and higher education magazine *Kariera*. *Kariera* is a weekly publication for the higher education community, prospective students and their parents. It offers articles on university life and education, comments on latest legislative and policy changes and initiatives, and publishes Russian university ratings. The collection of documents for factual information presented certain difficulties. In older institutions, the archiving and storing of departmental information was not consistent over time. While the events of the past five years were relatively well documented, accurate information about prior years was harder to find.

The third and final phase of data collection was completed during the fall of 2003. During Phase 2, I began to build the cases, overlapping data analysis with data collection in order to make adjustments to the latter (Eisenhardt, 1989).[2] Therefore, Phase 3 consisted primarily of additional document gathering for the purposes of clarifying the findings from Phase 2 and member checks. For instance, the data gathered from the documents in Phase 2 did not provide enough information to create a coherent picture of the social, political, and economic context of the study. In order to fill this gap, I scanned the front pages of the popular weekly *Argumenti i Fakti* (AIF) for 1989–2003 (the total number of issues: 720). AIF publishes analytical articles about economic, political, and social reforms in Russia. Its front page is known for its concise summaries of major events covered in the issue and its satirical political collages, capturing the spirit of the week. In this study, AIF served not only as a record book of major historical events in Russia, but also as a reflection of changes in the state discourse about the economy and economics.

DATA ANALYSIS

Twenty-five interviews were recorded on audiotape at USU, MSU, and HSE (nine, eight, and eight interviews, respectively). The interviews were translated into English and transcribed. The translation was author-oriented rather than reader-centered. The reader-centered translation implies taking into consideration the features and preferences of the targeted audience, whereas the author-centered approach requires that translators take into consideration the author's context and intentions in producing the text (Hatim & Mason, 1990). Given that the purpose of the interviews was to solicit respondents' opinions and perceptions grounded in their personal experiences and contexts, I believed the author-centered translation was more appropriate for the study. To ensure the anonymity of the respondents, their names were removed from the script. The accuracy of the translation was evaluated by a qualified Russian-speaking peer.

The transcript of the translated interviews was imported into a qualitative software program (NVivo), examined, and coded for stories. Borrowed from literary studies, my definition of a story was based on the understanding that whenever "there is an action or an event, even a single one there is a story because there is a transformation, a transition from an earlier state to a later and resultant state" (Genette quoted in Herman, 2002, p. 27). Thus, a story in this research project is defined as a fragment of a narrative (interview) that describes actions, events, and experiences that led to, resulted from, or involved change in an initial state or situation. In the context of the study, by the initial state I understood the domination of Marxist political economy in economic education and research. Temporally, this state corresponded to the Soviet period (1917–1991).

For the purpose of analysis, the stories were codified by topic. The results of coding by topic for three universities are presented in Appendix C. The stories were then examined for enthymemes. Once I identified the enthymemes, I analyzed them for a missing part (a premise or a conclusion) and reconstructed to the complete syllogism structure: major premise; minor premise; and conclusion. The reconstructed missing premises and conclusions represented taken for granted, or controversial knowledge that the respondents assumed in their narratives. Next, the reconstructed sentences were abstracted from the three-part syllogisms and arranged in a list, which was imported in a qualitative software program (NVivo), examined for themes and coded. As a result of the coding, several categories emerged. Among the categories common for all three universities were design of new programs and courses, adoption of Western methods and practices, adaptation of Western material to local contexts, problems with old faculty, characteristics of good faculty, and Soviet traditions.

Not all of the stories and enthymemes were accepted for analysis. As a result of the extraction of stories from interviews and the reconstruction of enthymemes, the volume of amassed qualitative data was immense. Facing the danger of what Pettigrew wittily described as "death by data asphyxiation" (Pettigrew, quoted in Eisenhardt, 1989, p. 540), I designed three filters. The first and the second filters excluded personal stories and general philosophical speculations as unrelated to changes in economic education. The third filter discarded discussions of the conceptual core of the discipline as material that is beyond the scope of this investigation. The results for each step of the rhetorical analysis are summarized in Table 3.2 below.

Table 3.2. Results of the Rhetorical Analysis

University	Recorded Interview	Story	Enthymeme Sentence
Higher School of Economics	8	76 (60 analyzed & 16 excluded from analysis)	198 (169 analyzed & 29 excluded from analysis)
Moscow State University	8	64 (51 analyzed & 13 excluded from analysis)	168 (148 analyzed & 20 excluded from analysis)
Ural State University	9	99 (89 analyzed & 10 excluded from analysis)	298 (271analyzed & 27 excluded from analysis)
Total	25	239 (200 analyzed & 39 excluded from analysis)	664 (588 analyzed & 76 excluded from analysis)

The documents were analyzed in two capacities: as artifacts bearing values and images of institutional culture and as sources of data for triangulation of information from the interviews. In their first capacity, only university documents were accepted for analysis: academic plans (*uchebnii plan*) of economics departments, course syllabi, minutes of the academic council meetings, university publications and newsletters, and university websites. The artifacts were examined for predominant themes, and categorized according to their foci. As the result, the documents were divided into four groups, signifying institutional excellence, faculty qualifications, integration into world academic community, and collegial and democratic spirit. The groups were compared across the three universities and the insights from the comparison were used to inform the integrative case analysis.

In their second capacity—as sources of information, the institutional documents were used together with the two above-mentioned periodicals, *Kariera* and *Argumenti i Fakti*. (For the list of documents employed in the construction of the cases, see Appendix B). The cross-case comparison of curricula and syllabi presented some difficulties. In order to establish a common ground for comparison and assess the closeness of Russian curricula to their Western analogues, I used a classification of economics designed by the *Journal of Economic Literature* (JEL). The idea was to assess to what extent the universities represent all fields of economic science in their organizational structures.

However, not all of the courses at Russian universities were readily translatable into the JEL classification. The HSE curriculum was closest in resemblance. As a young university based on Western models of education, HSE patterned its economics curriculum on Western European programs and therefore used similar course titles. Moscow State and Ural State curricula had slightly different combinations of general education and economic courses. Similar difficulties occurred in comparing specializations of economic departments at Russian universities with the JEL classification.

MEASURES ENHANCING THE QUALITY OF DATA COLLECTION AND ANALYSIS

I took several measures to enhance the quality of data collection and analysis. First, following Grunow's (1995) suggestion about the internal consistency of the design, I was mindful of the interrelationship between my research question, method, and the social constructivist orientation of my theoretical framework. Second, during the interviews, following Tashakkori and Teddlie's recommendation (1998), I checked for interviewer effects on responses where possible, by asking clarification questions in the follow-up or post-interview conversations. Third, as described earlier, I invited a peer to evaluate the accuracy of my translation.

Fourth, drawing on Feldman and Sköldberg's (2002) experience in identifying stories and enthymemes, I sought a peer's assistance during stages of the rhetorical analysis. The peer with a background in literary studies read through the stories and enthymemes and helped resolve ambiguous cases.

Fifth, following the recommendations of Newman and Benz (1998) and Stake (1995), I kept a journal with reflections and insights throughout the duration of data collection and analysis. The journal recorded observations of the situations and circumstances in which the interviews were conducted, contextualizing the respondents' answers, and collected thoughts about particularities of the linguistic translation of the interviews, contributing to the understanding of the process of organizational translation.

Sixth, I created an audit trail in the form of transcribed interviews and collected documents, which were used to triangulate the data gathered during all stages of the project (Crewswell, 1994; Stake, 1995). Finally, I conducted member checks with my respondents in Russia and peer debriefing with my colleagues in Russia and the U.S., particularly with regard to the cases (Stake, 1995; Yin, 1989). The purpose of the member checks and debriefing was to ensure that the cases avoid distortions in the presentation of people and events.

While the above-mentioned measures serve to enhance the construct validity and internal validity of the study, they do not address the problems of replicability and external validity. The criterion of replicability requires that the findings be consistent over time. Since repetition of interviewing and document analysis is beyond the scope of the proposed study, replicability of findings is one of the limitations of this research project. The issue of external validity or generalizability of qualitative research is a topic of contention among social scientists. While some scholars insist that this criterion is applicable to qualitative studies (Miles & Huberman, 1984, 1994; Tsoukas, 1989; Yin, 1989), others believe that it is not (Denzin & Lincoln, 2000; Guba & Lincoln, 2001; Numagami, 1998; Marshall & Rossman, 1995; Symon & Cassell, 1998). As a comparative case study of adaptation of one discipline, the results of this research have limited statistical generalizability to other disciplinary fields. However, this study intends to generalize not to other academic fields, but to theory. Put differently, the study is concerned not with statistical but with analytic generalizability (Yin, 1989). From this perspective, the research is valid: the methods and the theoretical framework are suited to each other, ensuring that the findings contribute to the development of theory.

Chapter Four

The Higher School of Economics: A Western University Model in Russia

This chapter presents a brief overview of the Russian system of higher education, highlights major events in the development of economic education in that country, and introduces the first case in the study: the Higher School of Economics. In the case, I offer an account of HSE events assembled primarily from HSE documents (syllabi, academic plans, university brochures, newsletters, and websites) and reflecting the narratives officially recognized and accepted by the University. The information from the periodicals *Kariera* and *Argumenti i Fakti* is used to place the described events in a larger social, political, and economic context. The case is supplemented with an analysis of HSE stories and enthymemes. In this part of the chapter I draw exclusively on the interviews to present the three most prevalent organizational stories and examine organizational beliefs and assumptions expressed in the enthymemes uncovered in the stories with the help of the rhetorical analysis technique. The stories highlight salient features of the HSE organizational identity as it is projected in the respondents' narratives. The enthymeme elements reconstructed as the result of the rhetorical analysis represent taken-for-granted knowledge and assumptions underlying the HSE faculty and administrators' participation in the development of economics at their university. This tacit knowledge illuminates the symbolic aspect of transformations taking place at HSE and complements the accounts of change presented in the first part of the case.

I conclude the chapter with an analysis that brings together the insights from the case, stories, and enthymemes. The analysis is framed by the institutionalist conceptualization of translation explained earlier in the book. Specifically, I focus on the following translation processes: transformations in organizational space, changes in organizational time (history), and rationalizations of innovations. The goal of the analysis is to explain the material (structure, practices, procedures) and symbolic (meanings) change processes that occurred at HSE as the school was adopting and adapting economics.

ECONOMIC EDUCATION IN RUSSIAN UNIVERSITIES: BACKGROUND OF THE STUDY

The Russian System of Higher Education

According to the State Committee on Statistics (Goskomstat, 2002), the Russian system of higher education consists of 1008 institutions of higher education that serve 5.4 million students. Slightly more than a third of all institutions are private (410), accounting for more than ten percent of the total student population in Russia (Lewis, Hendel & Demyanchuk, 2003). Almost one half of all public colleges and universities are located in fifteen cities; and Moscow and St. Petersburg traditionally boast about a quarter of the total number of schools (Kitaev, 1994).

Historically, Russian higher education was patterned after the French and German systems. From the French, it took the element of centralized control. From the Germans it adopted the idea of a university as a center for the pursuit of pure knowledge separated from practice-oriented technical institutes (Bain, Zakharov & Nosova, 1998). Thus, Russian higher education is highly centralized with research being traditionally assigned to the institutes of the Russian Academy of Sciences (RAS). The vertical line of subordination requires that a university rector (president) report to the Minister of Education. Not all universities are governed by the Ministry of Education. Educational institutions preparing specialists for industry, agriculture, and the military are governed by their respective ministries. The power of the minister at the top of the hierarchy is mediated by the Rectors' Union, a professional association of the highest university leaders who lobby for their interests with ministries and the government.

While leading Russian universities such as Moscow State converted some of its programs to a Western system of a four-year baccalaureate and a two-year Master's, many universities still retain the Soviet degree system along with the new baccalaureate and Master's. The Soviet system consists of a five-year program leading to the Diploma of Specialist. The *kandidat nauk,* candidate of sciences (roughly an equivalent of an American PhD), requires at least three years of study beyond the Diploma of Specialist and research, culminating in the defense of a dissertation. The highest academic degree of *doktor nauk,* doctor of sciences, is awarded by a special national committee in recognition of outstanding and important research. The average age of doctors of science increased from 58 in the mid-1990s (Piskunov, 1996, p. 25) to 61 in the early 2000s (Reznik, 2001a). The increase is significant especially in the light of the fact that the retirement age for women in Russia is 55 and 60 for men.

In the mid-1990s, in the spirit of change and democratization, the Ministry begin to encourage the development of educational research that had been long neglected in the Soviet Union (Nikandrov, 1997) and sought the input of educational experts in the design of educational standards (Voogt, 1998). Starting in the mid-1990s, the Ministry also began to attract foreign experts for large scale studies of various educational policy issues. The World Bank, the Organization for Economic Cooperation and Development (OECD), and the European Union's Tacis Program sponsored several projects on primary, secondary, and tertiary education in Russia (Canning, Moock & Heleniak, 1999; OECD, 1998, 1999; White Book, 2000).

By the end of the 1990s, the Russian system of higher education had expanded to include tuition-based institutions and schools granting Bachelor's and Master's degrees. Marked as commercial in the political discourse, the new tuition-based institutions often became the subject of attacks on the part of opponents of marketization of education. At the same time, presumably non-commercial public universities were forced to respond to market pressures by opening new departments with popular disciplines, establishing public relations and marketing offices, and accepting a certain proportion of students for tuition.

In reaction to the market pressures and political changes in the country, in 1998–2000 a group of educational experts under the leadership of Rector of the Higher School of Economics, Kuzminov, and Minister of Education, Filippov prepared drafts of a proposal for educational reform. Referred to as Modernization of Russian Education, the reform proposed student loans, tax breaks for investors in education, and a new mechanism of higher education funding whereby student aid went not to universities as it had been practiced, but directly to students in the form of governmental individual financial obligations (GIFO), or vouchers (Klyachko, 2001; Kuzminov et al., 2002; Obrazovatel'naya politika, 2002). Furthermore, the reform also requested that the value of GIFO be tied to student performance on the unified state exit examination, which would replace entrance examinations organized by individual universities (Filippov, 2000; Kuzminov et al., 2002). Although eventually adopted by the parliament in 2001, "Modernization of Higher Education" was strongly opposed by rectors of several large universities, including the rector of the Moscow State University (e.g., Sadovnichii, 2000). The reform established principles of running higher education institutions in the market economy.

Economic Education in the Soviet Union and Contemporary Russia

Scholars studying the preparation of economists in the Soviet Union note that the Soviet economist had "less in common with an American economist than [did] American economists with American sociologists or other social scientists" (Alexeev, Gaddy & Leitzel, 1992, pp. 139). Indeed, unlike Western programs based on micro, macroeconomics, and econometrics, Soviet economic education was founded on three pillars: Marxist philosophy, Marxist political economy, and historical materialism (Ofer & Polterovich, 2000). Guided by Karl Marx's *Capital* as the main theoretical text, Soviet scholars regarded Western economics as a bourgeois science serving the needs of the capitalist system that would ultimately give way to more progressive socialism. Since Marx's writings included little mathematical calculation and modeling, Soviet economics relied primarily on descriptive institutional analysis.

The state-enforced isolation of the Soviet academics from the world academic community and the strict censorship of foreign books and journals entering the country did not permit Soviet economists to keep abreast of Western scholarship. The few copies of Western undergraduate textbooks that Soviet libraries received were kept in closed stacks and made available only to postgraduate students for the purposes of criticism. Those that were translated into Russian were edited. Gerschenkron (1978) relates how Samuelson's classic undergraduate textbook was translated into Russian in 1966 and in the process underwent a series of "corrections" that restated the Marxist postulate of the inevitability of the eventual demise of capitalism. The style of written publications in Soviet economics reflected this disregard of original sources and lack of empirical economic research. Ofer & Polterovich (2000) report that even in 1997, several years into reforms, half of the articles published in the leading economic journal, *Voprosy ekonomiki,* had only one or two references.

Though political economy dominated economic curricula, it was only part of the program. The program also included mathematics and statistics. Mathematical economics began to gain recognition in the Soviet Union in the 1960s and 1970s after professors L.V. Kantorovich, V.S. Nemchinov and V. Novozhilov were awarded the prestigious Lenin Prize for their mathematical modeling and Kantorovich shared the Nobel Prize in economics with Tjalling Koopmans in 1975 (Alexeev et al., 1992). Although comparable with Western economics, mathematical modeling had limited application to the Soviet reality. Along with other factors, fixed prices in the Soviet Union led to what Western economists characterized as "the economy of vast distortions" (Alexeev et al., 1992) where a standard analysis of the incentives, costs and benefits of a proposed policy was discouraged if not impossible. Under these circumstances, according to the critics of the Soviet system, "the principal role of Soviet economists had been to explain why the policies which the state had already implemented were in fact optimal" (Alexeev et al., 1992, p. 138). Economic statistics was similarly flawed: it used unreliable economic data provided by the State Committee of Statistics (Goskomstat), which itself was under political control and censorship (Ofer & Polterovich, 2000).

Yet, the complex vocabulary and mathematical basis of the "system analysis" and economic cybernetics offered mathematical economists some refuge from political control. Claiming that mathematical research is value-free, they had a greater freedom in studying the works of their Western peers who also relied heavily on mathematical modeling. This familiarity with Western scholarship proved crucial later in the 1990s when, during the transition to a market economy, the Russian government realized that it needed well-trained economists with a knowledge of the market system (Stuart, 2000). Ironically, the other group of economic faculty who would later be sufficiently qualified to teach mainstream economics were those who taught courses on the criticism of capitalist systems and bourgeois theories (Ofer & Polterovich, 2000).

Adaptation of Western economics by Russian universities in the early 1990s had extensive ramifications in terms of organizational structure and culture as well as epistemology. First of all, the faculty of the existing programs in economics were trained in Marxist political economy and often espoused views that were in conflict with the premises of Western economics. Commenting on this situation, Brue and MacPhee (1995, p. 189) observed that assigning old faculty to teach courses in economics was "like assigning a creationist to teach evolution." While some faculty who had been trained in political economy decided to learn mathematics in order to continue teaching economics, some moved to other social sciences. Yet others changed the titles of their courses and continued to teach the old content under a new name. Such was the case of Scientific Atheism[1] that continued to be taught at Moscow State economics programs under the guise of World Religions until the mid-1990s and may still be taught in other universities.

Training and re-training of faculty, therefore, became key to the successful introduction of Western economics in Russia. In 1992, the Economic

Development Institute (EDI) of the World Bank launched a program for government officials in order to familiarize them with the principles of a market economy. The program for the officials was preceded by a series of re-training seminars for leading professors of political economy. Held in Washington D.C., the seminars were organized by the World Bank and the International Monetary Fund (Kovzik & Watts, 2001). As a result of these re-training programs, the Moscow EDI office and Moscow State University (MSU) Retraining Institute supported a group of MSU professors who translated several Western textbooks and wrote Russian textbooks on economics (Kovzik & Watts, 2001). Long regarded as a leading Russian university, MSU has also been instrumental in disseminating economics by designing one of the first comprehensive curricula in mainstream economics with the help of Western experts.

Changing existing programs was not the only way of introducing economics in Russia. Newly trained market economists often try to avoid the old established institutions because of low pay and excessive control by administrators. Creating new institutions, particularly joint ventures with Western universities has become an effective alternative to restructuring old schools (Ofer & Polterovich, 2000). Perhaps, the most successful example of this second approach is the New School of Economics (NES) created as a partnership between the Central Economics and Mathematical Institute (CEMI) of the Russian Academy of Sciences, the Hebrew University in Jerusalem, and Moscow State University with financial support from the Soros Foundation. Since it opened its doors in 1992, the NES has managed to become a center for original research on transition markets, creating a new branch of economics—economics of transition—and demonstrating that its curriculum is not a direct imitation of Western programs but an adapted product (Pleskovic et al., 2000). The establishment of a branch of economics that is directly related to the post-Soviet economy is a remarkable achievement, given the fact that the majority of the translated textbooks utilize American and European examples, which to Russian students may read "like the study of life on the planet Mars" (Ofer & Polterovich, 2000).

Like all social science research in Russia, research in economics is hindered by low funding and a lack of advanced literature. To remedy the situation, the Economics Education and Research Consortium (EERC) was founded in Moscow in 1996 to provide grants, workshops, seminars, as well as a publications program to foster high quality research in economics. The EERC has an annual budget of $1 million and is run by an advisory committee of leading Western economists (Pleskovic et al., 2000). Today, research and teaching in economics in Russia is also supported through a number of Western programs and organizations. To name a few, the granting organizations include the European Union's Tacis Program, the Eurasia Foundation of the U.S. government, Higher Education Support Program of the Soros Foundation, the Ford, MacArthur, and Carnegie Foundations, the Know-How Fund of the British Government, and several Scandinavian foundations (Ofer & Polterovich, 2000).

Despite the wide-spread introduction of economics in Russian university curricula, scholars analyzing the status of the discipline in that country note that the old barriers remain a "strong legacy of Marxist political economy education, weak connections with the world economic community, poor financing, and brain drain" (Ofer & Polterovich, 2000). The situation is further complicated by the fact that the dissemination of Western economic ideas is happening at a time when some segments of the population may become increasingly disappointed with the results of market reforms and feel antagonistic toward the West. In the communist and nationalist discourses specifically, the market principles are associated with exploitation and westernization, hence erosion of Russian culture (McAuley, 1997).

Summary

The system of higher education in Russia consists of public (state) and private universities and teaching institutes as well as the Russian Academy of Sciences with its research institutes. The system is characterized by centralized control, separation of research and teaching, and an uneven geographical distribution of institutions in European and non-European parts of Russia. Most public higher education institutions charge tuition fees, although a certain proportion of students study for free. To varying degrees, most universities employ both Soviet (Diploma of Specialist) and Western (Bachelor's and Master's) program designs.

The introduction of economics was accompanied by ideological and structural changes in Russian universities. Establishing new courses and programs in economics, Russian academics experienced a lack of financial and information resources and the resistance of their colleagues and administrators trained in Marxist ideology. Western European and American universities and organizations played a significant role in supporting the introduction and development of the discipline in Russia. The World Bank was instrumental in establishing the first economics courses in the country, while international philanthropic foundations supported much of the research and changes in economic education.

A HOUSE BUILT FOR ECONOMICS: THE CASE OF THE HIGHER SCHOOL OF ECONOMICS

First Attempts to Create a Program in Economics

At the end of the 1980s, the Soviet Union embarked on a series of political and economic reforms that would ultimately lead to its dissolution in 1991 and to the beginning of a long transition toward a market economy. While the country's planned economy was being rapidly eroded by market forces, Russian universities continued to teach courses on the economy of socialism, thus preparing students for the economic system that was disappearing (Ofer & Polterovich, 2000).

At the time, Moscow State University was not only the largest and most prestigious university in the nation, but also the best model of Soviet higher education. The government generously provided for the needs of the university and its faculty who belonged to the Soviet cultural and financial elite. MSU students were also outstanding, having passed rigorous MSU entrance examinations. Regarded as the crème de la crème in their academic fields, MSU graduates went on to occupy teaching positions at the best universities in the country and were eagerly hired by the prestigious Russian Academy of Sciences[2] research institutes.

As a nation's intellectual center, MSU fostered a spirit of critical thinking. The Economic Faculty at MSU prided itself in developing a culture of independent thinking among its professors and students. Officially channeled to criticism of capitalist economy and science, the habit of critical analysis bore fruitful results in generating theoretical constructs and models that drew on or were friendly to Western science. Such was Kantorovich's work on mathematical modeling of economic processes that earned him the Nobel Prize and opened new directions for Soviet research (Alexeev et al., 1992).

It was in this spirit of independent and critical thinking that several MSU faculty members gathered together in 1989 to think about how to make economic education relevant to the on-going transition to the market. The group consisted of a few senior faculty, notably, Evgenii Yasin, Revold Entov, Oleg Ananiin, and Rustem Nureev, and a handful of young lecturers and docents led by Yaroslav Kuzminov. Coming from the best university in the country, this group of colleagues had the abilities and the desire to introduce Western economic approaches to Soviet education and apply them to the study of the Russian economy in transition. Together they decided to design new courses based on Western economic theories.

Yaroslav Kuzminov quickly established himself as a leader of the project. In 1989, he was leaving his position as a lecturer at the MSU Department of History of Economy and Economic Thought for an appointment as a junior researcher at the RAS Institute of Economy. By that time, he had had ten-years of teaching experience at MSU, co-authored several influential textbooks on the history of economic theories, and established a reputation as an exceptional scholar with expertise in Western economic thought. Kuzminov was also known for his rather openly critical attitude toward the classics of Marxist thought. His former students still recall the awe that they felt when they listened to the charismatic young lecturer who critiqued Friedrich Engels's *Anti-Düring*. Suggesting the fallibility of the Marxist theory was heretical enough, but pointing out where it was fallible was outright bold and Kuzminov had the reputation of a young and daring pro-Western scholar.

Evgenii Yasin also assumed responsibility for the project. A full professor at MSU, in 1989 he was appointed to a position at the State Committee on Economic Reforms housed at the USSR Council of Ministers. Actively involved in the practice of transforming the Soviet Union into a market economy, he made no secret of his dissatisfaction with the Marxist doctrine. Yasin's political views and his position in the government piqued the MSU administration. The differences between Yasin and the administration would soon become irreconcilable and he would be forced to leave the university.

Looking for a place in the curriculum for new courses, Kuzmin and Yasin believed the MSU Economic Faculty and particularly the Department of Political Economy within it had been too slow and reluctant to question the supremacy of Marxism and include Western theories into the curriculum. They came to believe that in order for them to design and teach new courses, they had to be structurally independent from what they perceived as conservative MSU Economic Faculty. Thus, they decided to organize an alternative department of economic theory.

The Kuzminov-Yasin group made two attempts to create an alternative department. First, in 1989 they organized a department at the Physical Technical Institute (or Phys-Tech, as it is abbreviated in Russian), an elite Soviet institute known for its physicists. With a small grant from the Soros Foundation, Kuzminov, Yasin, and their colleagues designed several courses based on Western economics and taught them for a year until the department was closed in 1990. After their undertaking failed to take roots at Phys-Tech, it was followed by another attempt in 1990 at the MSU Faculties of Physics and History. The second attempt met the same fate as the first and the department was closed down a year after it was opened.

Although the alternative departments were short-lived, they yielded important results. First, the group set a precedent in designing a cycle of courses based on Western economic theories, which until then had been considered "false science" by all universities in the country. Second, using Russian reforms as examples, they began to develop methods of teaching transitional economics, thereby adapting Western theories to the post-Soviet context. Third, the alternative departments produced future cadres for the Higher School of Economics: upon graduation several years later, their students would form a nucleus of the HSE faculty.

Nurturing the Idea of a New University

Disheartened by the failure of the alternative departments at Phys-Tech and MSU, Kuzminov and Yasin became convinced of the need for a new university based on Western models of education. They envisioned a small state institution—a school of higher learning—that would prepare Masters in economics. In 1991, facing strong opposition from MSU, the two began to promote the idea among government officials. During his work at the State Committee on Economic Reforms, Yasin made connections at the Council of Ministers. Employing that network to promote the idea of a new school, he found enthusiastic supporters in several highly influential political figures: Prime Minister Yegor Gaidar, Minister of Labor Alexander Shokhin, and Academician Leonid Abalkin. Plans were made to establish a school under the auspices of the Academy of Science.

The year of 1991 was a turbulent one for Russia. A failed coup d'état by the communists in the summer, the dissolution of the Soviet Union in the winter, and a virtually paralyzed economy contributed to the political and economic instability. In these circumstances, Kuzminov and Yasin decided to explore alternative sources of funding outside of Russia and approached the European Commission with a proposal for a new educational institution in economics. In 1992, the EU awarded them a large grant to organize the school and in November of the same year, the Russian government issued a document formally establishing the Higher School of Economics as a Master's granting state educational institution.

Building a School From Ground Zero

HSE was created deliberately and ostensibly in contrast to the existing Soviet universities, MSU in particular. In his historical notes on HSE, Kuzminov (Higher School of Economics, n.d.) described the School's mission as three-fold. First, HSE had to become a "university that supports creative self-realization of its members." Second, it had to "re-build the connection with the *world* economic science" by preparing new economists and scholars of economics. Third, it had to "distribute *normal* economic knowledge and introduce it in the academic and bureaucratic spheres." Thus, from the beginning, HSE was charged with the task of correcting what, from Kuzminov's and Yasin's experiences at MSU, appeared to be the stifling of creativity, parochialism, and the bad science of Soviet universities. "We will build a Harvard of Russia in economics," Lev Lyubimov, the first Dean of HSE Economic Faculty, used to say—pointing out that contrary to the official Soviet discourse, the best education model was not MSU and was not even in Russia but in the West.

Before the School opened its doors to students, Kuzminov and Yasin had a year to find a building to house classrooms, hire faculty who could teach economics, design a Master's program, prepare syllabi, print teaching materials, and attract students. The call for faculty spread by word of mouth in the Moscow academic community. Kuzminov and Yasin telephoned their friends and colleagues inviting them to teach at HSE and asking them to recommend others. Former students and colleagues at the alternative departments at Phys-Tech and MSU were a natural first choice, making up a large proportion of the candidate pool. Thus, most of the first HSE faculty either knew each other by acquaintance or were friends. Most importantly, however, they all shared Kuzmin's and Yasin's vision of the new school and were willing to exchange the stability of their faculty and research appointments for vague prospects of a higher salary and intellectually stimulating yet effortful work at HSE.

Although the newly hired faculty were familiar with world economic theories and had some degree of mathematical preparation, they were mostly self-taught in Western academic subjects. Given the scarcity of texts on economics in the Soviet Union, the results of their self-education would not be sufficient for teaching at the Master's level. Therefore, in the School's first year, HSE faculty became students again, but this time to a small group of Russia's best academics who were invited to lecture on a range of subjects in economics.

While the enthusiasm about creating a Master's program was high among the faculty members, few actually had an idea about how to design a program. In March 1993, the HSE applied for and received another grant from the European Commission. The Tacis Program grant started a three-year partnership among HSE, the Erasmus University of Rotterdam, Holland, and the Russian Ministry of Education. The purpose of the partnership was to design the HSE curriculum and train the faculty. Six months into the project, HSE designed a curriculum, created textbooks for students, wrote teaching guides for the faculty, and invited international scholars to teach select courses. By September 1993, the School was prepared to receive its first students and about a hundred of them entered HSE in its first Master's class.

Formative Years

Starting in 1993, HSE faculty began to travel regularly to European universities. They took courses in economics, worked in the libraries, and learned how programs in economics were organized in the West. In 1994, in addition to the Erasmus University, HSE partnered with Gent University in Belgium and the University of Hamburg in Germany on a year-long project to design new courses and establish visiting lectureships for international academic economists.

The year of 1994 was also marked by several events that would significantly contribute to the School's growth in the years to come. Evgenii Yasin was appointed the Minister of Economic Development. Despite his demanding new position, Yasin decided to stay on the faculty and take part in HSE governance in his capacity as the School's supervisor for academic affairs. The same year, under Yasin's influence, HSE acquired a second supervisory body. From then on, in addition to the Ministry of Education, Rector Kuzminov had to report to the Ministry of Economic Development. Besides new responsibilities, the double subordination brought the good will of a powerful ministry and its human and financial resources. Furthermore, in 1994 the School got a home of its own—a century-old building in the center of Moscow.

The ministerial officials as well as policy makers, industrialists, and bankers became regular guest lecturers at HSE, supplying a practical application component to the theoretical content of the curriculum. As the result of their engagements at the School, the Ministry, Russian and international banks, firms, and corporations began to view HSE students and graduates as desirable candidates for internships and employment. The Russian company LogoVAZ established fifteen student scholarships. The consulting firm Arthur Andersen established ten and signed an agreement to admit HSE students for internships. Students themselves began to seek international contacts and build networks. In 1994, they formed a local organization of the international student association AIESEC (Association Internationale des Etudiantes en Sciences Economiques et Commercials). As members of AIESEC, they gained professional links and access to international exchanges between employers and students of economic disciplines.

From the inception of the School, the French Ministry of International Affairs had been HSE's active supporter. In fact, the grant that founded HSE was co-signed by the French government. In 1994, HSE and French universities, Paris-I and Panteon-Sorbonne, started a collaborative research project that two years later would lead to the establishment of a French university consortium supporting HSE. To coordinate the increasingly complex projects with France, in 1996 HSE created a non-academic Department for Cooperation with France. French involvement in the foundation and development of HSE was so great that it prompted Michail Sollogub, a faculty member at Paris-I, to call HSE a French-Russian child.

Growing Into the World Academic Community

Expansion of the Economic Faculty

During its first two years of 1992–1993, HSE had a lean structure with a handful of departments: Economic Theory, Mathematics and Econometrics (transformed into Mathematical Economics and Econometrics in 1999), Applied Macroeconomics, Theory of Money and Credit, and Institutional Economics and Economic History. Although the official founding dates of these departments are 1992 and 1993, respectively, in practice they formed long before the School was established. The faculty members who made up the nuclei of these departments often had a shared history of collaborations in math, institutional economics, or economic history.

In 1994, three more departments were created: State Administration and Public Economics, Regional Economics and Economic Geography, and Investment Markets. In 1995, HSE was upgraded to the status of a university and *State University* was added to its name. As a university, HSE was now able to open faculties in other disciplines.

In the meantime, the Economic Faculty continued to grow and restructure. In 1995 Institutional Economics and Economic History was reorganized into Institutional Economics. The same year, the Department of Economic Sociology was created only to be reorganized into the Department of Social Economic Systems and Social Policy four years later. The Departments of Banking and of International Accounting and Auditing appeared in 1996. In 1999 HSE organized faculty members teaching statistics into a separate Department of Statistics and created the Department of Applied Microeconomics. In 1999, the Department of Risk Management and Insurance appeared. In 2001 the Department of English Language split along disciplinary lines and the Economic Faculty founded its own Department of English for Economics. The same year, the Department of the

Table 4.1. HSE Economic Faculty Departments and Corresponding Economic Fields

Department	Economic Field
Economic Theory	A. General Economics & Teaching
Economic Methodology & History	B. Schools of Economic Thought & Methodology
High Math for Economics; Mathematical Economics & Econometrics; Statistics	C. Mathematical & Quantitative Methods
Microeconomic Analysis;	D. Microeconomics
Macroeconomic Analysis; Theory of Money and Credit	E. Macroeconomics & Monetary Economics
Economy in Transition	F. International Economics
Economics of Firm and Finance; Investment Markets	G. Financial Economics
State Regulation of Public Finance	H. Public Economics
Not a separate department	I. Health, Education, & Welfare
Not a separate department	J. Labor & Demographic Economics
Not a separate department	K. Law & Economics
Applied Analysis of Industrial Organization	L. Industrial Organization
Banking; Accounting & Auditing; Risk Management & Insurance	M. Business Administration & Business Economics; Marketing; Accounting
(see Economic Methodology & History above)	N. Economic History
Not a separate department	O. Economic Development, Technological Change, & Growth
Social Economic Systems & Social Policy	P. Economic Systems
Agricultural Economics	Q. Agricultural & Natural Resource Economics
Regional Economics & Economic Geography	R. Urban, Rural, & Regional Economics
Institutional Economics State & Municipal Administration	Z. Other Special Topics
English for Economists	

Economy in Transition and the Department of Economic Methodology and History appeared, absorbing some of the faculty from the old Department of Institutional Economics and Economic History. The Department of Applied Analysis of Industrial Markets was opened in 2002. The year of 2003 saw the establishment of four more departments: High Mathematics for Economics, Macroeconomic Analysis, Economics of Firm and Finance, and Agricultural Economics, which was formed from the former Applied Microeconomics. By 2003, the Economic Faculty had 22 departments. Thus, in ten years, the School gradually adopted virtually all fields of economic science as they are known in the West[3] (see Table 4.1 for the list of the HSE departments and corresponding economic fields).

New academic faculties and collaborative projects

While France remained its most important partner, HSE explored relationships with economists from other countries as well. Since 1993 it ran a project with Erasmus University of Rotterdam, Holland. In 1994, HSE negotiated a dual Master's degree with Erasmus. In 1996, when HSE received its status of university, it opened two more faculties: the Faculty of Management and the Faculty of Law. Double degree agreements with French universities gave HSE Master's students in economics, management, and law an opportunity to study simultaneously for the Russian Master's and French national diploma DEA (Diplôme d'études approfondies). In 1997, the School commenced a thirty-month project with the University Paris-Defance, the University Paris-X, Nanterre, the French company SODETEG, the French State Council, and the University of Essex, Great Britain. The project supported the development of programs, courses, and teaching materials on law and economics and funded HSE faculty and students to study these disciplines in Europe. In 2001, HSE and Humboldt University in Berlin, Germany, launched a joint Master's program in economics.

The increasing flow of collaborative projects and exchanges exceeded the functional capacities of the Protocol Department, a bureaucratic structure created during the School's first year to organize and service faculty and student exchanges, international conferences, and meetings. In 1997, HSE opened the Student Mobility Advisory Office, and a year later the Department of International Travel, Visas and Registrations. As HSE expanded the geography of its partnerships, in addition to the Department for Cooperation with France, there appeared the Department for Cooperation with Germany and the Department of Prospective Projects that explored HSE connections in North America.

The subsequent grants, partnerships, and collaborative projects allowed HSE to expand its academic structure and branch out into other cities. In 1996, on the invitation of the Governor of the Nizhniy Novgorod Region, the School opened a branch in Nizhniy Novgorod, the fourth largest city in Russia. In 1997, two more branches were created in Novosibirsk, Russia's fifth largest city and Siberia's academic center, and in Perm. In 1998, after restructuring the Academy of Shipbuilding and absorbing Telecom Institute for Professional Enhancement, HSE opened a branch in St. Petersburg.

In 1997, together with the London School of Economics, HSE began a project that culminated in the opening of the International Institute of Economics and Finance (IIEF). The IIEF offered joint Russian-English programs in several economic specializations and awarded Bachelor of Arts degrees from the London School of Economics and from HSE. In 1998, HSE created the Faculty of Applied Political Science. In 1999, the School reorganized its sociology program into the Faculty of Sociology, opened the Faculty of Psychology, and with a grant from the World Bank began a three-year project to design three new Master's programs in microeconomics, institutional analysis and politics; macroeconomics and econometrics; and economics of public sector and public policy. In 2002, the Faculty of World Economy and Faculty of Business and Informatics (computer science) received its first students. Plans were made to open the Faculty of Public Administration and the Faculty of Philosophy in the fall of 2004.

Thus, in ten years the Master's program with a hundred students grew into the Faculty of Economics with 1,500 students in baccalaureate, Master's and PhD programs. Having started as one faculty, the School grew into ten faculties in various disciplines and three branches in other cities. The Moscow campus expanded to eight large buildings, a hotel for foreign visiting lecturers, and three student dormitories.

Retraining the Economy's Leaders

First through Yasin's and Kuzminov's professional networks, then by virtue of its links to the Ministry of Economic Development, HSE had been closely connected to a circle of Russian economic reformers from the time of its founding. The year of 1997 marked a turn in the development of HSE when this connection evolved into a series of projects that would establish the School as a center of expertise in various fields of national economy and as an active participant in state policy making.

In March, 1997, together with the Amsterdam Academy of Banking and Finance and Bureau CROSS, Holland, HSE began a project to re-train bank managers. In November, the School started another international project. This time, with the assistance from the Caledon University in Glasgow, Scotland, it designed programs for retraining managers of non-governmental retirement funds. Furthermore, in 1997 the Russian Government made HSE the main national retraining center for procurement executives, leading to the establishment of the Institute for Training of Specialists in State Procurement. And finally, in 1997 HSE began a project to improve the performance and efficiency of the Ministry of Economy.

By 2003, HSE had twelve more training centers and institutes for government officials, managers, bankers, and businesspeople, including a program designed specifically for the Ministry of Economy and an executive MBA. Despite the steadily growing tuition fees, HSE's programs continue to increase by a thousand entrants each year.

Economic Research

In addition to retraining Russia's government officials, bankers, and executive officers, HSE became a center for applied economic research on Russia. The research at HSE is organized through four institutes (Social Policy, Pricing and Regulation of Natural Monopolies, Macroeconomic Research and Forecast, Enterprise and Market Studies) and five centers: Educational Policy, Environmental and Natural Resources Economy (established together with Harvard's Institute for International Development), Corporate Governance (together with Schulich School of Business of York University in Canada), Human Rights, and Labor Research. Combined with research on economic education and teaching, in 1998–2003 HSE's 660 full-time and 450 part-time faculty members published 140 monographs and 450 textbooks and study guides.

Outreach in Economic Education

As a pioneer in Western economic education, in the early 1990s HSE experienced difficulties in selecting students for its baccalaureate program. Indeed, leading universities in the country had just begun establishing contacts with economics departments abroad, and several tiers down the system secondary schools existed in complete isolation from communities of economists. As a consequence, graduates of secondary schools had little exposure to basic economic concepts and theories. To remedy the situation, HSE opened a teacher-training center, identified and selected feeder schools that offered economics, and organized preparatory courses. By 2003, the number of the secondary schools affiliated with HSE reached 79.

In addition, in 1994, HSE received a four-year Tacis grant to study and improve teaching of economic and business disciplines at secondary and technical schools, and universities. Initially, the project involved nine universities from Russia's three regions. In 1998–2001, a follow-up Tacis grant expanded the number of university participants to sixteen and resulted in the creation and publication of sixteen new Russian textbooks and teaching guides in economics for secondary schools and universities. In 2000, HSE formed a consortium with the Ministry of Education, the Moscow Committee on Education, Erasmus University in Rotterdam, the Institute of Education of the University of London, Trinity and All Saints Leeds University (the UK), and departments of education in three Russian regions for retraining educational administrators. Thus, HSE became integrated in the secondary school community and established professional networks with other Russian universities offering programs in economics.

Rivalry with Moscow State University

The rapid development of the School did not go unnoticed by Moscow State University. For several years, the continuously expanding HSE had been successfully recruiting its faculty from the MSU professoriate. By 1998, the student enrollment at HSE Economic Faculty equaled in size the enrollment at MSU Economic Faculty. For the first time, the Moscow State Economic Faculty had a serious competitor comparable in size and reputation.

The rivalry brought big and small victories to both sides. Among HSE's undoubted successes was its appointment as the head university at the Teaching and Methodological Association (in Russian abbreviation, UMO) for economics and management. Appointed by the Ministry of Education, a UMO serves as a gateway to a disciplinary field: it develops disciplinary standards, determines the content and boundaries of disciplines, approves or disproves of the latest scholarly developments, benchmarks best practices in teaching and scholarship, recommends manuscripts for publication, and endorses textbooks for use in the classroom. Although officially they serve in an advisory capacity to the Ministry, the power of the UMO is so strong that the Ministry would not authorize educational standards without their endorsement and publishing houses would not publish textbooks without their stamp of approval. To be appointed head of the UMO for a particular discipline means controlling the way this discipline is taught and developed for the entire country. As Russia's leading university, MSU has housed several UMOs in different disciplines and academic fields, including economic theory. Therefore, when in 1996 HSE was appointed as the head university for the officially approved specialization of economics and management, the School welcomed it as an establishment of a power balance between MSU and HSE.

The tension between MSU and HSE heightened in 1998–2000 when the HSE Center for Educational Policy prepared a project for educational reform. Entitled *Modernization of Russian Education,* the project proposed a new funding mechanism for education and a unified state examination system that would lead to the abolition of individual university entrance exams. Advocated by HSE Rector Kuzminov, the project was strongly opposed by MSU Rector Sadovnichii. After months of debates, *Modernization of Russian Higher Education* was adopted as law by the Russian Parliament and the School strengthened its position as a policy maker in Russia.

Epilogue

In 2003, more than a decade after its foundation, HSE continued to develop as a state university with a strong research and policy-making component. Structurally, it reproduced Western university models with their division into Bachelor's, Master's, and PhD programs and credit-hour system. HSE actively expanded its international peer networks: in 2003, the School became a member of the European University Association and joined the OECD Institutional Management in Higher Education program. The leanings of the HSE leadership to liberal economic policies did not go well with conservative politicians and leaders in education. HSE's ties with Western universities and organizations are not interpreted to the School's advantage when its Rector advocates market-based approaches to reforms in education. Three years after Kuzminov's *Modernization of Higher Education in Russia* became law, the staunchest of his opponents still called him an agent of the West, while the West, represented by the French government, awarded him with the prestigeous Order of the Academic Palm (l'Ordre de la Palme Académique).

HSE STORIES AND ASSUMPTIONS:
THE WORLD ACCORDING TO HSE

Supplying mostly factual information about the development of the School, the case only begins to explain the symbolic processes that took place at HSE. For instance, the history of antagonism between the School's founders and the MSU administration accounts in part for today's rivalry between the two universities. However, what is not clear from the official account is to what extent this rivalry is reflected in the ways HSE envisions adaptation of economics. Moreover, besides suggesting that the HSE faculty and administration share pro-Western intellectual leanings, the case explains little about how these pro-Western orientations influenced the development of the Faculty and the curriculum for a decade. Finally, acknowledging the importance of Yasin's and Kuzminov's roles as HSE founders and leaders, the case offers only glimpses of their symbolic significance to HSE's organizational identity. The stories and enthymemes help answer these questions and recreate beliefs, values, and tacit understandings that underlie the world of HSE respondents.

The eight interviews with HSE faculty and administrators contained 76 identifiable stories. As described earlier, by a story I understood a fragment of a narrative (interview) that described actions, events, and experiences that led to, resulted from, or involved the adaptation of economics by the university. Sixteen stories were excluded from analysis as irrelevant to the study: they either contained personal life stories or speculations about possibilities of a theoretical synthesis of Marxist political economy and Western economic theories. The remaining 60 stories were coded by topic. The results of the coding are presented in Appendix C.

Sixty HSE stories were inspected for enthymemes. Having identified enthymemes, I then analyzed them for missing premises or conclusions. As a result of this examination, 198 omitted premises and conclusions were found and reconstructed. Twenty-nine of the reconstructed enthymeme parts were eliminated as irrelevant to the analysis: they also contained personal references or involved arguments about a theoretical synthesis of Marxist political economy and Western economic theories. The remaining 169 reconstructed enthymeme premises and conclusions were coded by themes. The results of the enthymeme coding for HSE are presented in Appendix D.

The foundation stories (n=11), accounts of the founding of HSE, were by far the most popular among the respondents. In three instances, the HSE respondents turned to the topic of the School's beginning and presented a second iteration of the events. An example of a such story is presented below. A HSE faculty member, one of the active participants in the initial development of the School, recalls:

> [The founding of HSE] was curious, it was remarkable. There was a desire, perhaps, a bit romantic desire to create a normal university according to a European model, because from the very beginning we charged ourselves with the task of creating a university in Russia where teaching of economics will meet the world standards, because not a single university in Russia at that time had been doing that and even until now almost no one has done that either. The situation hasn't improved

much and in some ways, it is even getting worse in some universities. Many leading universities in the country are in deep crisis in terms of economic education. So the idea was to collect the leading people [in economic science] from different places, people who are not corrupted by work in Soviet higher education, and to create a university where one could prepare normal specialists who are not tortured by Marxist-Leninist political economy and who know the contemporary economic theory and are capable of working in new structures of the Russian economy. It was a rather romantic desire. So a group of enthusiasts gathered together. People came from different places. Not all of them came from universities, many came from the Academy institutes, many came from various research centers. . . . Such was the group of enthusiasts who created a new educational institution out of absolutely nothing. There was no building, no program, no nothing. We created everything ourselves from zero.

This is a story par excellence: it contains heroes (a group of enthusiasts), foes (Soviet universities that "torture" students with Marxist-Leninist political economy), the rags (the protagonists had "absolutely nothing," "zero" at the beginning), and the riches (HSE today is a "normal university" that "prepares normal specialists" "according to the world standards"). The protagonists appear larger-than-life in their power to create a university out of nothing. They stand out as romantic and truth-loving rebels who challenge the academic world corrupted by the Marxist-Leninist ideology and attempt to right the Soviet wrong (or to normalize it). The heroes overcome great difficulties building a university from ground zero and their trials culminate in the foundation of HSE. In short, the story of the School's beginning is what Clark (1972) called an organizational saga.

Clark (1972), who studied organizational sagas in higher education, observed that they serve as powerful transmitters of organizational values. Sagas not only tell organizational members what their organization is like, but also show them what they should be like as organizational members. In other words, sagas foster the construction of a unified organizational identity. In the HSE foundation stories, the story-tellers express their pride in the School's roots and demonstrate their solidarity with the founders' struggle and cause. In doing so, they re-enact the persistent antagonism between the old Soviet academic establishment symbolized by MSU and pro-Western free-thinking academics personified by HSE leaders and propagate this antagonism as an organizational value.

The enthymeme parts reconstructed from the stories further illustrate tacit assumptions that the members of HSE have about their school, and its relationship to old large state universities such as MSU. HSE faculty and administrators believe that new universities are founded by idealists. They take it for granted that collegiality is essential to new universities as well as good leadership, faculty's common educational background, and a good library. Good leadership is defined as innovative and entrepreneurial. Good leaders are expected to respect student views about curriculum and seek faculty opinions on institutional development.

HSE faculty and administrators presume that old universities are unattractive to young faculty, do not welcome change in higher education and pressure their faculty to use old approaches in course design. They also assume that small schools like HSE are more creative than large schools like MSU and that the number of innovations is a measure of institutional quality. The founding of HSE is regarded as a sign of revival in Russian economic education. The School is believed to promote new standards, to want change and to employ only those faculty who went through proper retraining in economics. Furthermore, the School is perceived as more progressive than MSU due to its advocacy of massification of economic education. It is taken for granted that HSE is respected by Russia's regional leaders, that it fights corruption while other universities do not and that it has better money-making opportunities for faculty than other universities. Moreover, HSE respondents believe that at present, MSU is threatened by the Higher School of Economics. While they take it for granted that in the Soviet Union, MSU was a good university with excellent faculty who had taught students critical thinking skills, they assume that MSU had a monopoly on economic education and favored children of high party officials.

The Soviet past is interpreted with mixed feelings by HSE faculty and administrators. As the enthymeme analysis reveals, they believe that Soviet education prepared bad economists for a market economy, that Soviet criticism of Western economic theories was irrational and Soviet interpretations of Marxism were out-dated and intellectually-stifling. Working at Soviet universities was believed to corrupt faculty and being anti-Marxist was seen as a sign of courage. On the other hand, HSE respondents presume that the Soviet courses on the history of foreign economic theories were intellectually stimulating and studying Lenin's works was educational. In addition, in contrast to what is perceived as a problem today, the government in the Soviet Union solicited opinions of the entire economic community.

Another group of most frequently told stories involves accounts of faculty members' traveling to Western Europe to study economics and use libraries to design courses for HSE (n=6). The account below exemplifies a story about traveling to the West to study economics:

> We have good and capable faculty, and as faculty, we had a lot of trips abroad. We studied at the Erasmus University, and at the Sorbonne, and at the London School of Economics, of course. It is not so much the coursework but the books that we could bring from there that were important, because it was impossible to buy anything here [in Russia] and all first knowledge that came here came in English. So we brought originals in English, read them, translated them, and then used them in teaching until our own courses were finally designed.

This story establishes a connection between the quality of faculty and their training abroad ("we have good faculty" and "as [good] faculty, we had a lot of trips abroad") and suggests the excellence of the HSE faculty education abroad: in addition to the Erasmus University and the Sorbonne, the list of illustrious institutions necessarily ("of course") includes the London School of Economics, which is arguably the leading economics center in Europe. The story also comments on the history of scarce information resources in economics in Russia: the HSE faculty members studying in Western universities placed more value on the books than on the knowledge they acquired abroad.

HSE stories about traveling to study abroad contain a host of tacit beliefs and assumptions about institutional and program quality where the quality is measured by or in association with the West. As the enthymeme analysis shows, HSE faculty and administrators presume that in order to open a new university one has to write a grant, go abroad, study Western models, copy Western models, and retrain faculty according to Western standards of education. Sending students to study abroad and practicing Western standards of education are understood to be signs of the university's quality and integration in the world academic community. HSE respondents also assume that in order to design a good program or a course in economics, one has to study with foreign teachers abroad or in Russia, know English, read foreign literature in the field, have an Internet connection at home to access foreign journals and university sites, and imitate Western models. It is taken for granted that Western models of economic programs are superior to those in the Soviet system. Western academic communities in general are seen as sources of authority: university administrators who are recognized by Western academic communities are valued as good leaders.

Similarly, the quality of faculty is understood as a function of their exposure to Western ideas and practices. HSE faculty and administrators assume that studying abroad makes one an expert and that in order to be able to study abroad, one has to have good academic preparation and intellectual ability. Studying economics in the West where the discipline is believed to be "taught properly" is important because only those faculty members who are taught properly are viewed as capable of producing scholarship at the international level. HSE respondents believe that good faculty members adapt textbooks of increasing difficulty in their course designs and make their students read original texts. Thus, it is taken for granted that in order to become a good teacher at a university, one has to study in the West first and than teach at home.

At the same time, whether faculty members studied economics in the West or at home, when they design courses in the discipline, their individual study skills and the knowledge that they can acquire on their own are seen as ultimately more valuable than the time they spend learning economics in the classroom. Thus, faculty members' continuous learning is taken as a sign of their professionalism. It is for that reason that the use of basic rather than advanced textbooks by faculty is assumed to be a sign of their low professional preparation, and the teaching of old courses on Marx's *Capital* is regarded as a sign of not learning new things. Incidentally, HSE respondents assume that it is old faculty, especially Marxist political economists, who are unlikely to be capable of learning economics, and that a preponderance of old faculty in a department is an indicator of a weak program and a barrier to institutional change. The problem of senior faculty not learning economics is expected to be solved in the long run by the change of generations: it is believed that in order for the new to take root, the old knowledge has to die out.

The third most frequent story in the HSE narratives is an account of re-training at home (n=5). Chronologically, this type of story begins at the founding of the university and is typically associated with the foundation saga, as a faculty member's account illustrates:

> So when I came here, HSE was very small. And look how many buildings we have now. One can get lost among them now: there is a building here and there is another one over there. But at that time the school didn't have its own building at all. Gaidar gave us shelter in his institute, we had several rooms there, and we had several rooms in another institute on the Prospect of Academician Sakharov, but the enthusiasm was amazing. We had few students then and we had few faculty, we all knew each other. We had little experience, we had little knowledge of *those economic theories*—my God, we knew almost nothing then—and our professors [names withdrawn]—and they are very well respected in the West—they organized lectures for us on economic theories and on math, and we tried hard to learn everything fast and there was an

atmosphere of unity, an atmosphere of enthusiasts who wanted to build
something without a building, without [established] faculty.

Like foundation sagas, this story contains romanticized recollections of the
esprit de corp of the School's first years ("an atmosphere of unity, an
atmosphere of enthusiasts") and contrasts the initial hardship and humility
("the school didn't have its own building" or established faculty, "Gaidar
gave us shelter") to the present prosperity and pride ("And look how many
buildings we have now. One can get lost among them.").

The story also presents an account of faculty learning economics at
home both in a national and organizational sense: while faculty members
at other Russian universities could not afford traveling abroad and
worked hard to get admitted to the few retraining programs organized
by the World Bank at the Moscow State, the HSE faculty benefited from
the expertise of the leading Russian professors versed in economics who
came under one roof to establish a new Western style university. By
returning to the student desk and voluntarily subordinating themselves
to the authority of their expert colleagues, HSE faculty members showed
their disregard for the formal hierarchy of academic ranks that requires
strict differentiation of student and professor roles and that is typically
associated with old well-established universities like MSU. By demonstrating the importance of knowledge acquisition over the maintenance
of organizational status, HSE faculty confirmed their commitment to
continuous learning and professional development. Although they
learned economics from Russian rather than Western professors, the fact
that their Russian teachers were "all very well respected in the West"
legitimizes their knowledge as authentically Western and therefore good
and appropriate for HSE.

The stories about traveling abroad and going through re-training at
home contain assumptions about the influence of faculty members' geographical location and foreign language proficiency on their capacity to
learn economics. As the enthymeme analysis suggests, HSE respondents
presume that to learn economics one has to study it like a student or work
as a graduate student assistant to a foreign lecturer in the discipline. They
take it for granted that today retraining in economics occurs both abroad
and in Russia and that learning advanced levels of the discipline requires
money for courses and travel. For that reason, teachers in non-European
parts of Russia are believed to be not learning the discipline at advanced
levels. Furthermore, it is understood that learning the discipline is supposed
to be easier if one reads translations of Western textbooks.

In the HSE narratives, discussions of the use of Western originals and their Russian translations are interwoven with the theme of applicability of Western content and methods to teaching in Russia. HSE faculty and administrators suppose that adapting foreign courses requires applying their content to the Russian context. However, they believe that the content of Western economics may not be relevant to Russia because of its overemphasis on mathematics at the expense of political and institutional analyses. HSE respondents believe that in order to enhance the relevance of economics to the real life in the country, universities should write new textbooks rather than translate foreign texts and invite experts from industry, business, and government as lecturers. In teaching economics, according to HSE administrators and faculty, one has to present the material without a Marxist bias and it is desirable to use the Western practice of written exams because written evaluation tools are assumed to be more objective than oral exams practiced in the Soviet Union.

Thus, the stories contain various assumptions and tacit knowledge about organizational roots, curricular design in economics, MSU, the Soviet tradition, and so forth. The rhetorical analysis of the stories brings these assumptions and tacit knowledge to the forefront, revealing a different text or a sub-text behind the case that describes the events recorded in official university publications (see Figure 3.1 for the relationship between the case and stories and enthymemes in the analysis).

The stories and reconstructed enthymeme premises and conclusions enrich the case with the insights about the HSE organizational values and taken-for-granted knowledge that underlies the actions of HSE faculty and administrators. The overview of the stories reveals the symbolic significance of the School leaders as founding fathers of the university. The stories about them communicate the HSE values of institutional autonomy, independence, and pro-Western sentiments. The reconstructed enthymeme elements demonstrate that the pro-Western orientations of HSE faculty not only permeate their thinking about education but also shape their ideas about program and course design into a mental model of action. The model consists of steps appropriate for each stage of university development: e.g., to start a program go abroad, study Western practices, copy Western practices; to design a course go abroad, work in the library, study foreign literature, etc.

The HSE rivalry with MSU is reflected in the respondents' understanding of the School's development strategy. HSE is understood to be the opposite of MSU with its ageing faculty and large organizational size. First, since old professors are believed to be unable and unwilling to learn economics, the School is presumed to be a collective of young professors who learn and adapt economic disciplines. Second, because small size is associated with creativity and innovativeness, HSE is expected to remain compact in its structures, symbolically if not in reality.

The case analysis below brings together the insights from the case, stories, and enthymemes for a comprehensive examination of the HSE's translation of economics.

HSE CASE ANALYSIS

As Sahlin-Andersson and Sevón (2003) point out, when an idea or practice is translated in an organizational context, it first has to be decoupled from the temporal and spatial context in which it originated and initially developed. Then, the receiving organization provides a new context for the idea or practice, making it part of its own organizational time and space and modifying it to fit the organizational structure better. In the official discourse of the organization, the adoption and modification processes are rationalized as leading to improvements. Adoption and adaptation of economics by HSE follows this logic of translation. At the time of its founding and in the following years, HSE modified the spatial and temporal contexts of the Western discipline, and created a rationalization discourse around it. The following discussion elaborates these modifications and rationalizations.

Structural Changes: Modifying Spatial Context

Although HSE was conceived as a Western university and its founders had the luxury of choosing the structural model they preferred, they acted within the legal and institutional boundaries of the Russian higher education system. As a social institution maintained through universities, research centers, the legislature, budget allocations, etc., higher education imposes its rules of operation. The most obvious of these rules are perhaps, subordination to the Ministry and fulfillment of the National Standards of Education.

Control of the Ministry. In a strongly centralized system such as Russian education, subordination to the Ministry puts constraints on what rectors can do. For example, with its formula establishing the number of students per square meter of the classroom space, the Ministry puts a cap on the maximum student enrollment for every educational institution. Therefore, the School's acquisition of its own building in 1994 was essential to the HSE development.

Another mechanism of ministerial control over educational institutions is the Standards of Education. When the School admitted its first students in

1993, the fulfillment of the National Standards of Education was the condition that gave universities the right to award state diplomas. At the time, the state diploma was the only type of document recognized by employers to certify the completion of higher education. From the perspective of Western economic education, the existing Standards of Economic Education in Russia were unacceptable. Thus, from the beginning, HSE had to negotiate between the curriculum structure imposed by the Standards and its own vision of proper education in economics. Although the School never blended a Marxist curriculum with Western economics, its programs accepted some of the practices widely used by other Russian universities in the field of economic education. Specifically, to its curriculum HSE added applied specialized courses in accounting, auditing, and marketing, which are typically separated from economics in Western programs. Thus, in the process of its adoption by HSE, Western economics was decoupled from its Western program structure and fit into a customized mold created for it by the School.

Internal structuring and restructuring. If the School's environmental context affected the structuring of its economics program, the reverse influence of the disciplinary structure on that of the university was also true. Particularly in its first years, HSE developed by adding on levels and branches of economic specializations, following the structure of the Western discipline as a road map. To the Master's program HSE first added baccalaureate and then PhD programs. To economic theory it added international economics and finance. As programs grew in size, they split in two, producing new departments and specializations. Eventually, courses on management were divorced from economics and placed into separate programs.

The transformations of the School's internal structures ensured that HSE remained a welcome setting for further adaptations of economic fields at each stage of the institutional development. They also reflected HSE's belief in the benefits of small organizational size as opposed to the large size of MSU. In the logic of comparison, MSU's large size signaled its lack of creativity and stagnation. Paradoxically, when in 1998 the HSE Economic Faculty grew to the size of its MSU counterpart, the School's economists still perceived their Faculty as small and therefore innovative. Thus, the School's organizational beliefs about organizational size simultaneously reflect and support its restructuring strategies.

Geographic expansion. Perhaps, the most visible organizational change occurred in the School's geographic expansion. The eight buildings of HSE's Moscow campus are spread all over the city. Branches of HSE operate in three large cities in Russia. HSE even expanded to France, Germany, and Holland through joint degree programs and student exchanges. The joint degrees not only enhanced the prestige of HSE as a university but also validated the School's economic education, confirming that the modified and adapted version of economics in the HSE curriculum is indeed a legitimate economic program.

Replication of foreign space. While internal restructuring and geographic expansion represent material changes in the spatial context, the organizational rhetoric constructs space symbolically. In his statement, widely quoted at HSE, Dean Lyubimov claimed to be building a Harvard of Russia in economics, i.e., recreating foreign space together with the new discipline. The replication of space in this case is certainly figurative rather than literal: HSU intended to emulate the high quality of the programs, excellent faculty and tradition that characterize Harvard, rather than its architecture. Nevertheless, the metaphor creates a compelling image and defines the university as a Western organization. The enthymemes in HSE stories provide similar examples of thinking that seeks to recreate foreign space through imitation of Western academic programs, course designs, and teaching methods.

In addition to modifying the spatial contexts of economics and HSE, the School had to demonstrate a continuity of academic tradition, which would ensure the adoption of a foreign discipline. In other words, the School had to alter its temporal context.

Borrowing Other's History: Modifying Temporal Context

In the HSE mission statement, Rector Kuzminov stated that one of HSE's goals was to "rebuild the connection with the *world* economic science." To stress the salience of the point, he underlined the attribute 'world,' contrasting it to the existing Soviet economic science. Thus, from the time of its foundation, HSE disconnected itself from the Soviet academic tradition, disavowing its shortcomings and achievements.

It is not accidental that in the mission statement, Kuzminov calls for rebuilding the connection to the world science. Rebuilding implies a previous loss. As it follows from the statement, what was lost in Russia was the world economic science that had existed in Russian universities before the Revolution of 1917. In the HSE rhetoric this loss is caused precisely by the rise of the Soviet tradition. This dichotomized perception of Soviet and world traditions is well illustrated by the enthymemes. HSE stories abound in normative judgments of Marxist political science as abnormal, intellectually-stifling, and theoretically false.

However, as a new educational institution, the School did not have pre-Soviet roots to re-claim. Therefore, it looked for tradition outside of Russia and found it in the Western academic community. Identifying themselves as heirs and followers of the Western scholarly tradition, Yasin and Kuzminov effectively borrowed other universities' history as their own. In doing so, the School's founders grafted HSU on the time continuum of Western economic disciplines, creating a temporal context conducive to the development of this field in Russia.

Rationalized Adoption

The HSE mission statement explains the rationality of adopting a new discipline in terms of correcting an error in the production of economic knowledge in Russia. Kuzminov, the author of the text, underlines the word 'normal' as the quality of the knowledge that HSE intends to produce. Representing what is correct and appropriate in economic sciences, HSE puts itself in contrast to incorrect and inappropriate scholarship, which is presumably exemplified by old Russian universities like Moscow State.

This tension between the old and the new is emblematic of HSE worldview. While in the official discourse the new is explicitly connected with progressiveness and institutional development, the stories and reconstructed enthymeme premises and conclusions provide the other side of the position, by revealing the implicit negative assumptions about the old. Old faculty are said to be unable to learn new things. The predominance of senior faculty in a department is seen as a sign of its stagnation. Old Soviet teaching methods are bad and so is old Soviet education in general. Old universities are uninteresting as they prefer old teaching methods. In this sense, rationalized adoption of new academic fields is HSE's raison d'être. It was founded to bring improvements in economic education, or as a reconstructed enthymeme conclusion captures it, the foundation of HSE is a sign of revitalization of Russian economic education.

The next case in the study turns to the School's long-time competitor and examines how economics was adapted by Moscow State University.

Chapter Five

Moscow State University: Tradition in Service of Excellence

Unlike HSE, which is a small young university with a distinctly pro-Western orientation, Moscow State is the largest and oldest university in the country and an exemplar of the Soviet academic institution[1]. With its strong scholarly reputation, the MSU Economic Faculty is HSE's main rival. However, in contrast to HSE, MSU did not reject Soviet traditions but used them as a foundation for new programs in economics. Presenting the MSU case in this chapter, I replicate the structure of the previous chapter: the first part consists of an official account of MSU events, the second part examines stories and assumptions extracted from MSU interviews, while the third one offers a MSU case analysis.

A MEETING OF SOVIET AND WESTERN SCIENCES: THE CASE OF ECONOMICS AT MOSCOW STATE

Economic Education at MSU Before 1991

Historical roots and foundation of the Economic Faculty. Founded by the decree of Empress Elizabeth Petrovna in 1755, MSU is the oldest university in Russia. Although like many other universities of the time, MSU focused initially on teaching theology, medicine, and philosophy, it had also been known to offer courses in economic disciplines at least since the early 1880s. The University charter makes the first mention of hiring professors of political economy, statistics and rural housekeeping in 1804. By 1835, the University had a fully-fledged Department of Political Economy and Statistics, and by the end of the 19th century taught a wide range of subjects from political economy to economics of industry, agriculture, trade and transport to credit and finance.

The October Revolution of 1917 commenced a period of dramatic structural and curricular changes at MSU. Together with the public, the University administration and faculty had to decide which disciplines served the cause of the Soviet state and which did not. As the result, some courses were banned from the curriculum altogether, while others remained and prospered. After decades of uncertainty, plans were finally made to establish a faculty to prepare specialists for the Soviet economy. In 1941, the Economic Faculty was officially established at MSU and received its first 28 students. In its first year, the Faculty consisted of a department of political economy and employed six professors.

The MSU Economic Faculty in the Soviet Union. In the decade after World War II, the Faculty opened departments of Statistics, Agricultural Economy, History of National Economy and Economic Thought, Analysis and Auditing, Economy of Foreign Countries and External Economic Ties, and Industrial Economics. In the 1960s, the departments of Mathematical Methods of Economic Analysis, Planning of Natural Economy, Employment and Social Labor Relations, and Population appeared. In the 1970s, the Faculty organized departments of Economy of the Non-Productive Sphere, Organization and Method of Public Socialist Production Management, Economic Problems of Natural Resource Utilization, and the English Language. By the early 1980s, the student enrollment at the Economic Faculty reached 200 students.

For forty-five years, until the collapse of the Soviet Union in 1991, the MSU Economic Faculty (MSU EF) provided first-class economists for the Soviet state and served as a pillar of the Marxist theoretical approach. Although the "ideologically militant spirit" of the Soviet economic science placed constraints on the advancement of new research agendas (Kolesov, 2001, p. 6), it did not stymie the development of mathematical methods of economic analysis. It was these courses in math methods that in the words of the MSU EF Dean Vasiliy Kolesov "served as a bridge between the national economic science and the main current of the rapidly developing economic knowledge in [the rest of] the world" (Kolesov, 2001, p. 6).

Mathematical analysis and economic cybernetics. In 1960, in addition to political economy, the Economic Faculty opened a second specialization: economic mathematics. Two years later, the Faculty created the Department of Mathematical Methods of Economic Analysis. Opened through the initiative of a distinguished statistician Academician Nemchinov, it was the culmination of several years of his efforts to revive the school of economic mathematics in the Soviet Union. Together with two more departments opened within the next couple of years, the Department formed a core of the economic mathematical specialization that became known in the Soviet Union as economic cybernetics. Starting in 1964, universities all over the Soviet Union began to open their own departments of cybernetics. The size of cybernetics classes was always kept small. For instance, at MSU the number of political economy students was at least twice as high as the number of cybernetics students.

Since mathematics was considered apolitical, cybernetics escaped much of the ideological supervision that was practiced in other fields. Unsupervised by the State, mathematical economists had greater freedom in choosing their research agendas and had better access to Western scholarship in economics. This intellectual independence from the politicized Soviet academia and the small size of cybernetics programs made mathematical economists elite in the eyes of Soviet economists.

MSU Economists in Perestroika

In 1987, the Soviet leader Michail Gorbachev announced the beginning of social, political, and economic transformations that became known under the term *perestroika* (in Russian, 'restructuring,' 'reconstruction'). The goals of perestroika were to democratize the Soviet political system and revitalize the economy. By the end of the 1980s, however, it started to produce unexpected consequences. The political debates began to question the very institution of the communist party, and the economy showed no signs of recovery. It appeared that a transition from a planned to a market economy was imminent.

Although in the Soviet period the MSU EF did not prepare specialists in micro and macroeconomics, its professoriate had some expertise in capitalist systems. This knowledge was gained mostly from the courses in cybernetics and the critique of bourgeois economic theories. In 1989, the World Bank organized a series of seminars in economics for select Russian faculty and government officials. The first group of students to travel to Washington, DC consisted mostly of MSU faculty who wanted to study the disciplines that they had known only in general terms. The idea behind the World Bank seminars was to teach teachers of economics so that they could disseminate the disciplinary knowledge at home. Therefore when the MSU faculty returned from DC, they were charged with the task of designing retraining programs and courses for local academics, economists, and the MSU EF students.

The MSU EF and National Economic Reforms

Thus, in the early 1990s it appeared that with its developing expertise in economics, the MSU EF would take an active part in conceptualizing and designing economic reforms. By that time, it already had a dozen and a half departments, laboratories, and research centers studying branches of the national economy. In 1989, responding to the needs of the changing financial structures, it even opened a new Department of Finance and Credit. With the national economy heading for crisis, the MSU EF was aware of its responsibility as a leading authority on the Soviet socialist economy. This awareness was increased by the public who looked to professional economists for solutions to national problems. "Are academic economists to blame for all our troubles? Does the economic science have a concept of the nation's development?" questioned a popular weekly from the front page (Zhelnorova, 1990). However, the Soviet academic community was divided about the course of reforms. Neither universities, nor the Russian Academy of Sciences (RAS) Division of Economy had a coherent program of economic transition.

In the atmosphere of confusion and divisiveness in the academy, the Supreme Soviet of the USSR, the USSR Council of Ministers, and the President created their own research teams and charged them with the task of planning economic reforms. The teams were assembled from a handful of leading economists from RAS research institutes and universities, including MSU. In addition, in the fall of 1990 the Soviet Government invited expert teams from the IMF, OECD, and International and European Banks of Reconstruction and Development to consult on the reforms. The significance of the invitation was grave, yet ironic. Probably for the first time in its history, the Soviet Government asked experts on capitalism to mend an economy based in socialism.

Divide Between Academic Economists and Reformers

Isolated from the rest of the academic community, the researchers on governmental teams did not seek consensus with their peers as the scholarly norms would prescribe it. Moreover, the 1990 reform proposals suggested a deliberate eradication of socialist methods of production. Trained in Marxism, academic economists witnessed how the purpose of their life's work—the study of socialist economic systems—was becoming meaningless as the planned economy was being replaced by the market. In light of these developments, academic economists increasingly felt left out by the state and resentful toward those colleagues who joined elite expert teams and participated in the reforms.

A spirit of contention beset the MSU Economic Faculty along with the rest of the nation's universities. At the Department of Statistics, Professor Yevgenii Yasin caused a particular controversy. Yasin was one of the select few who were invited by the Council of Ministers to design economic reforms. In the fall of 1990, a group of economists led by Academician Shatalin presented their concept of economic reforms to the public. Shatalin's proposal (1990) included establishing private property, privatizing state enterprises, liberalizing prices, and decreasing centralized state control over the market. In short, it was the antithesis of what Soviet political economists envisioned for the economy. Yasin was one of the co-authors and co-signers of the proposal. After an unpleasant period of confrontation with the Faculty's administration, he resigned his position at the MSU EF and left the University. In 1992, together with a small group of colleagues from MSU, Yasin would found the Higher School of Economics and two years later go on to become the Minister of Economic Development.

Restructuring for Economics

Introducing Bachelor's and Master's. Even though the Faculty did not take a leading position in guiding national economic reforms, it indeed was the leader in adopting the Western two-level system of baccalaureate and Master's. When in 1989 and 1990, following the World Bank seminars, MSU professors began to design new courses in economics, the Faculty ran into difficulties in expanding the existing curriculum. The teaching of the curriculum was divided among the Faculty departments. Responsible for a particular curricular segment, each department saw the need to strengthen its portion with new courses reflecting the changing economy. At the same time, none was willing to relinquish old courses. Since most of the curriculum in the Soviet system was required, adding new courses meant increasing the student workload. Thus, by 1991, students in MSU economic programs were required to spend 36 to 40 hours a week in lectures and seminars. The program could no longer absorb additions without restructuring.

In 1991, at the meeting of the Faculty's Academic Council, the Faculty administrators and professors decided to transform the five-year specialist programs into a four-year baccalaureate and a two-year Master's program. The significance of that decision cannot be underestimated. The legislature that officially established the legality of Bachelor's and Master's programs would appear only five years later. In the meantime, the practices of the MSU EF would be emulated by hundreds of other universities in the country who would justify their innovation by the authority of Moscow State.

Structuring, restructuring, and renaming. The graduates of the Washington, DC seminars formed the core of faculty designing Bachelor's and Master's programs. At the same time, other faculty members sought opportunities to learn economics at the World Bank seminars in DC and Moscow, and engaged in self-education. While the foundations in micro and macroeconomics were easiest to learn and adopt for teaching, learning the various specializations of the economic discipline proved to be more difficult. As professors studied and created courses on industrial organizations, international economics, theories of firm, management, marketing, and other branches of economic knowledge, the Faculty's structural units underwent changes.

Most of the departments went through internal reorganization, revised course content, and changed priorities in research. To reflect the changes, several units made alterations in their names or, in the words of an MSU administrator, they 'clarified' them. For example, the Department of Industrial Economics became Industrial Economics and Foundations of Entrepreneurship. The Department of Planning of Natural Economy was converted to Macroeconomic Regulation and Planning. The Laboratory for the Complex Study of Economic Laws and Categories in Socialist Conditions lost its Soviet designation and became the Laboratory for the Study of Market Economy. And finally, the Department of Organization and Methods of Management of Public Socialist Production acquired a market orientation and became Industrial Management.

Since the existing structure could not accommodate all specializations of the economic discipline, in 1992 the MSU EF opened the Department of Employment and Social Labor Relations. In 1994, it created the Department of Economic Informatics. The Department of Risk Management and Insurance appeared a year later. Finally, in 2001, the Faculty opened the Department of Applied Institutional Economics, raising the number of labs and departments to 21, including three departments run collaboratively with the Academy of Sciences. By 2003, the MSU EF had about 3,000 students and employed about 350 full-time and 400 adjunct faculty, covering all economic fields as they are known in Western universities.[2] The list of the MSU EF structural units and corresponding economic fields is presented in Table 5.1.

Table 5.1. MSU EF Units and Corresponding Economic Fields

Department	Economic Field
Not a separate department	A. General Economics & Teaching
Department of Political Economy; Laboratory on Philosophy of Economy	B. Schools of Economic Thought & Methodology
Department of Statistics; Department of Mathematical Methods of Economic Analysis; Department of Economic Informatics	C. Mathematical & Quantitative Methods
Laboratory for the Study of Market Economy; Laboratory for the Study of Property	D. Microeconomics
Department of Macroeconomic Regulation and Planning	E. Macroeconomics & Monetary Economics
Department of Economy of Nations and External Economic Ties	F. International Economics
Department of Finance and Credit	G. Financial Economics
Laboratory of Economic Methods of Public Production Management	H. Public Economics
Not a separate department	I. Health, Education, & Welfare
Department of Employment and Social Labor Relations; Laboratory for Economics of Population and Demography; Departmentof Population; Center for the Study of Population Problems	J. Labor & Demographic Economics
Not a separate department	K. Law & Economics
Department of Industrial Management; Department of Economics of Industrial Organization and Foundations of Entrepreneurship	L. Industrial Organization
Department of Accounting, Analysis, & Auditing; Department of Risk Management & Insurance	M. Business Administration & Business Economics; Marketing; Accounting
Department of History of National Economy and Economic Thought	N. Economic History
Not a separate department	O. Economic Development, Technological Change, & Growth

Table 5.1 (continued). MSU EF Units and Corresponding Economic Fields

Department	Economic Field
(see Department of Economy of Nations and External Economic Ties above)	P. Economic Systems
Department of Agricultural Economics; Department of Economics of Natural Resources	Q. Agricultural & Natural Resource Economics
Not a separate department	R. Urban, Rural, & Regional Economics
	Z. Other Special Topics
Department of English	

International Collaboration for Excellence in Economic Education

In 1994, the MSU EF received a large grant from the European Commission for the purposes of faculty re-training, curriculum development, and textbook translation. The Tempus grant was awarded to MSU for six years. During the period of the project, the Economic Faculty partnered with the London School of Economics, the Sorbonne, and the University of Tilsburg, Holland for a number of activities. First, the British, French, and Dutch faculty were invited to MSU as visiting lecturers. Second, MSU faculty traveled abroad to study various economic fields. In addition to attending classes, they worked in the libraries and consulted with their academic supervisors on the issues of course design, selection of textbooks for translation, and adaptation of Western content to the Russian context. As the result of the exchange, the MSU faculty designed and implemented courses in ten economic specializations and translated several popular European textbooks into Russian. Finally, the grant purchased 700 books in economics in several European languages, thereby establishing a small but valuable library at the Faculty.

In 1997, the Economic Faculty officially adopted a new version of the economic curriculum, created in collaboration with Western universities. The curriculum closely resembled its Western counterparts in that it had micro, macroeconomics, and econometrics at its core, contained courses in several economic fields, and offered electives. In the fourth year of their baccalaureate studies, students were offered a choice of specialization in one of the six areas: economic theory; mathematical methods in economic analysis; financial economics; international economics; economics of the firm and industrial economics; and economic and social policy.

In 2000, the Faculty was awarded another Tempus grant. Entitled "Improvement of Higher Education in Economics at MSU," it had three goals: to revise and expand the curriculum, to re-train more faculty members abroad, and to purchase computers and equipment for multimedia classrooms. Specifically, it was decided that in the course of three years, the Faculty would design and introduce 30 new courses in several economic fields and publish 35 textbooks. For that purpose, approximately 100 faculty members would be sent abroad to study, work in libraries, and consult with European professors. Additionally, a group of faculty would travel to the University of Navarra's IESE Business School, Spain, to learn case methods.

In addition to the large European Commission grants aimed at improving education, the MSU EF departments established individual collaborative research partnerships and projects. By 2003, the list of the Economic Faculty's partners and collaborators included 11 universities in North America, 7 universities in Germany, 7 higher education and research institutions in France, 3 universities in Great Britain, 2 universities in Holland, 2 institutions of higher learning in Spain, 2 universities in Switzerland, 2 universities in Sweden and 2 in South Korea. Furthermore, in Belgium, Bulgaria, the Czech Republic, China, Finland, Israel, Ireland, Italy, Japan, Poland, and Yugoslavia, the Faculty had collaborative projects with at least one leading university.

Strengthening Leadership at Home

Having designed and implemented a new curriculum, the MSU EF directed the grant money into the organization of summer schools and workshops for instructors of economics from other universities. In two years, from 1999 to 2000, the Faculty re-trained 109 academic economists from approximately fifty Russian universities. The Faculty also became involved in the development of MSU branches in Sevastopol, Russia, and in Astan, Kazakhstan.

Besides retraining Russian faculty in economics, MSU disseminated models and practices in economic education through its leadership at the Teaching and Methodological Association (UMO) for Classical Universities in economics. The group of classical universities consists of predominantly old, large universities with a comprehensive range of programs in the humanities, and the social and natural sciences. Universities with a narrow professional orientation, such as Higher School of Economics, are not included in the group. Since in the typology of Russian universities, the classical university is often regarded as the most prestigious, its programs, models, and practices are emulated by other educational institutions. To be the head university of a UMO in a discipline or specialization means essentially being responsible for the disciplinary content and structure in the entire territory of Russia and participating members of the Newly Independent States (NIS). Therefore the MSU EF influence on the development of economic education in the former Soviet Union is great. Within the framework of the UMO, the MSU EF cooperated in economics with three universities in the Ukraine and with one leading university in Belorussia, Armenia, Georgia, Uzbekistan, Tadjikistan, and Kyrgyzstan, covering a large NIS territory from Europe to the Caucasus to Central Asia.

An integral part of University life, the Economic Faculty supported Rector Sadovnichii in his critical assessment of the current reform in higher education. Following Sadovnichii, EF Dean Kolesov voiced strong opposition to the Rector of the Higher School of Economics Kuzminov, the reform's author. The confrontation between the two rectors and two philosophies of education became particularly poignant in March 2004, when Minister of Education Fillipov, Kuzminov's strongest ally, resigned and the new Minister decided to wait before taking sides.

Epilogue

The MSU EF remains a most prestigious and selective center for economic education in Russia. A high passing grade on the Faculty entrance exams is maintained and out of five applicants only one is admitted to the program. The MSU EF professoriate is one of the most degreed in the country. More than half of the full-time faculty have a candidate of sciences degree (an equivalent of a US PhD) and an additional 18 percent are doctors of sciences.

With a vast geography of research collaborations, the MSU EF enjoys a good reputation among peer institutions in the world. At the same time, the Faculty prides itself on the Soviet tradition of political economy. Reflecting on the place of the MSU EF in the world history of economic thought, a Faculty website states:

> The deep historical roots of political economy at Moscow State University, in Russia, and in the world in general made it possible to preserve the tree of economic knowledge until the present 21st century, while the rich scholarly legacy of economic scientists of the past centuries formulated fruitful grounds for the continuation of scientific inquiry by contemporary researchers. (Mezhdunarodniy symposium, 2004)

MSU STORIES AND ASSUMPTIONS: THE WORLD
THROUGH THE PRISM OF TRADITION

The Moscow State case demonstrates how an adherence to Soviet traditions by the Economic Faculty was a barrier to organizational and curricular changes at the initial stages of adoption. At the same time, the case suggests that Soviet traditions served as a foundation for adapting the new discipline. The rhetorical analysis of MSU stories casts light on this paradoxical finding and helps explain how Soviet traditions can function both as a conservative force and a source of change.

The eight interviews with MSU faculty and administrators contained 64 identifiable stories. Fifty-one stories were accepted for analysis, whereas thirteen were excluded either as irrelevant to the discussion or as exceeding the scope of the study. The stories were examined for common topics and coded. The full list of the stories, coded by topic, is presented in Appendix C. The rhetorical analysis of 51 stories from MSU interviews generated a list of 168 reconstructed enthymeme premises and conclusions. Twenty were discarded as containing personal references. The remaining 148 were examined for themes and coded. The results of the enthymeme coding for MSU are presented in Appendix E.

As it follows from counting stories on the same topic, most often MSU respondents shared accounts of traveling to the West (n=6) and adapting Western content to the Russian context (n=6). The stories of traveling to the West are exemplified by the account below. Explaining how the majority of his/her colleagues were able to study abroad, the author of the story shows pride in the accomplishments of his/her department.

> Indeed at the Moscow State, we adopted a personnel policy that . . .
> placed the main emphasis on studying, so to speak, Western disciplines,
> the Western version [of the disciplines] by all professors. That is why
> practically all of the faculty members of our department went to the
> universities in the U.S. or to the universities in Europe where they stud-
> ied and learned these disciplines locally. So I repeat, there is no faculty
> member who hasn't been either to U.S. universities or to European uni-
> versities, because besides cooperation with American universities, we
> had collaborations in the European Union's Tacis-Tempus program and
> our faculty members went to France, the Netherlands, Germany—it is
> difficult to enumerate all the countries where our faculty members have
> been. So practically, all of them went through re-training in the univer-
> sities where these disciplines are taught locally. That is the first trend
> [of the personnel policy] that allowed us to smoothen the painful tran-
> sition from the Marxist political economy to contemporary courses.

In this story, traveling to the West is presented as a conscious effort on the part of the department to turn its faculty into experts with authentic knowledge of the Western discipline. The authenticity of the acquired knowledge is stressed by the emphasis on learning economics "locally" in its native environment. The scope of the department's undertaking is equally impressive: the participation of faculty ("practically all of the faculty members of our department," "there is no faculty member who hasn't") is as broad as the geography of their travel ("it is difficult to enumerate all the countries"). Furthermore, the story implicitly acknowledges the organizational crisis at MSU caused by the necessity to replace the old Marxist curriculum with the Western discipline: study abroad programs are prescribed as medicine to alleviate the organizational ailment ("to smoothen the painful transition").

The enthymeme analysis of MSU narratives brings to light some of the tacit beliefs and assumptions behind the MSU policy to have its faculty educated abroad. Much like their HSE peers, MSU respondents assume that in order to design a good program in economics, one should first travel to the West to study that discipline. To learn economics, one has to know a foreign language, have access to foreign publications, especially to the originals, and have a good background in mathematics. Like HSE faculty and administrators, MSU respondents believe that in order to learn the discipline well, one has to study it like a student, that the advanced levels of the subject can be learned only in a foreign university, and that self-education is a viable alternative to education in the classroom.

MSU faculty and administrators share some of the assumptions about faculty generational differences with their HSE peers. For example, MSU respondents also presume that senior professors are unlikely to be capable of learning new disciplines; that younger faculty are quicker at learning economics and more creative in teaching it; and that younger faculty studying economics abroad contribute to organizational development, while a preponderance of senior faculty is as a sign of organizational stagnation. However, despite being criticized for its ageing faculty, the MSU Economic Faculty prides itself on employing accomplished senior scholars, assuming that it has achieved a balanced ratio between the older and younger faculty, which is beneficial for its programs. Furthermore, the size and location of a university are implicitly tied to its faculty members' ability to adapt economics: faculty at large universities located in the center of the country (Moscow and St. Petersburg) are believed to make the transition to the new discipline faster.

Traveling abroad for study and collaboration with the West in general shapes MSU ideas about institutional improvement. The symbolic significance of the University's interactions with the West is illustrated by the assumptions about organizational survival and development. In order to survive and be accepted by the world academic community, MSU economic programs have to adopt the Western content and methods of economics. Educating faculty abroad is seen as key to MSU's survival and interactions with foreign universities are believed to be beneficial for change inside MSU. Similarly, at the departmental level, having faculty educated abroad is regarded as essential to internal transformation. Moreover, the quality of a department is correlated with the number of faculty who studied abroad, and the quality of new programs is believed to depend on collaboration with Western organizations.

Another most frequent story in the MSU narratives is an account of the adaptation of Western economics to the Russian context (n=6). A faculty member explains how the content of his/her syllabus changed over time:

> Well, at first, the Western authors accounted for almost one hundred percent [of the syllabus], because my subject had been formed in the West and in order for me to learn it, I had to start with the Western originals. Now the portion of Western sources has decreased because first of all, our Russian authors have learned it already and begun to do research on their own, and second, one wants not just to study the way it is [in the West] but also to apply it to what you see here [in Russia]. So the proportion of Western texts in my work has decreased. Of course, when I am on a study abroad, I read mostly Western authors, but when I am here, the ratio is fifty-fifty, I believe. So the proportion of Western authors has decreased.

This account reinforces the tacit understanding that a good professor should be able to read original texts in their native language—the assumption common both to HSE and MSU narratives. As the rhetorical analysis of other stories on the topic reveals, MSU faculty and administrators assume that working in the libraries abroad is a prerequisite of designing a good course in economics, and that it is appropriate to study Western models before designing a new program or changing the existing one. They also assume it is normal to copy Western models in the design of study guides and other supplemental materials to textbooks but the textbooks themselves have to be adapted to the Russian context. Including Russian textbooks in course syllabi, such as described in the excerpt above, is believed to be a solution to the problem of limited relevance of the Western content to the Russian economy.

An examination of MSU stories across topics reveals an additional feature of the MSU narratives. Fourteen stories (on eight topics) have a distinctly common temporal dimension: they refer to the Soviet Union. Furthermore, nine of them have a strong evaluative quality, describing Soviet education in terms of excellence, and one of the stories about a conflict between Western and Soviet methods suggests the superiority of the latter. Since Moscow State University is known for its reputation as the leading university of the Soviet Union, the stories about its Soviet past deserve a closer examination. An MSU faculty member's recollection of his/her studies and work during the country's transition from socialism to capitalism is a typical example of stories about the excellence of Soviet academic traditions:

> In the 1980s, when I went to [Moscow State] University, we were taught Marxism only. We went to the University in one country, but [after graduation] we went to work in a completely different country. I meet my classmates now—250 of us graduated [from the MSU EF]—and none of them got lost in life. They all say in unison the same thing, "Even if the concrete knowledge that we acquired here turned out to be useless, we learned a much more important thing: we were given the culture of thinking, we were taught how to think, how to search for knowledge, how to process and systematize it, and how to use it." So here we were taught general principles and skills to acquire and work with knowledge and when the old knowledge turned out to be useless, we already knew where we should go for new knowledge [in economics], how to process it, how to synthesize it and inscribe it in our existing picture of the world, and how to use it. . . . The strength of the Soviet academic education is that it teaches you how to think, it gives you the culture of thinking, and we, who went to school in one society and began careers in a completely different one, we were prepared for that change.

This story exemplifies a common assumption for MSU narratives that the content and the quality of Soviet economic education was such that it laid foundations for the future transition to economics and market thinking. In addition to illustrating the belief in the superiority of the Soviet education, the story describes the mechanism of knowledge acquisition. It suggests that new ideas do not replace the old ones completely. Instead, new knowledge is "inscribed" in the respondents' "existing picture[s] of the world," combining the elements of the new and the old together. Furthermore, the reconstructed enthymemes of similar stories suggest that the old view is still in operation at MSU: MSU respondents assume that Marxism is a viable theoretical approach applicable to the analysis of contemporary phenomena and that political ideology does not diminish the value of Marx's seminal work, *Capital.* At the same time, they take it for granted that the political economy of socialism is not a legitimate discipline, while economics is.

The tension between the old Soviet traditions and new Western practices is further illuminated by the rhetorical analysis of the MSU stories about the Soviet past. While Western programs in economics are viewed as sources of useful organizational models, Western curricular designs and teaching methods are subjects of controversy. MSU respondents presume that the Soviet system of organizing curriculum by topic is better than organizing it by introductory, intermediate, and advanced levels as it is practiced in the West. Furthermore, Western courses are assumed to be the complete opposite of Soviet in-depth specialized seminars and are therefore judged as superficial. Similarly, the Soviet emphasis on in-classroom as opposed to individual learning and the role of teacher as presenter of processed knowledge are viewed as signs of good education and contrasted with Western teaching methods. Perceived dichotomously, Western methods and practices are believed to be destructive of the superior Soviet methods. Even the Western system of written tests and examinations, which is perceived as an improvement of objectivity in evaluation, is regarded as an assault on the Soviet tradition of oral presentation. Yet, the beliefs about the inferiority of Western methods coexist with the understanding that Soviet teaching methods are outdated and that in order to teach economics, one has to use Western teaching methods.

The stories and the reconstructed enthymemes suggest that adherence to the Soviet traditions is one of the central features of MSU's organizational identity. Given the history of the University, the symbolic investment in the tradition is not surprising. However, what is remarkable is that it does not preclude the importation of Western practices. The assumptions about the inferiority of Western methods coexist with Western-oriented mental plans of program and curricular design: MSU faculty and administrators take it for granted that the source of economic knowledge is located in the West and so are the models of economic programs. Furthermore, the rhetorical analysis shows that MSU respondents perceive their connections with Western universities in terms of survival and change. Despite the perceived inferiority of Western practices, collaboration with the West brings enough resources and prestige to be seen as contributing to rather than diminishing the quality of the MSU EF programs.

MSU CASE ANALYSIS

The Moscow State University case has no heroes championing Western disciplines. Unlike the Higher School of Economics, the MSU Economic Faculty did not have leaders with a compelling vision and a radical plan of action. In fact, there is some evidence to the contrary: in the early 1990s, when the Faculty faced the problem of an overblown curriculum, the administration could not persuade the departments to relinquish their old courses. The departments chose not to share the vision of the Faculty leadership and pursued their own courses of action. Yet, the MSU EF did accomplish change, retraining its professoriate, adding new departments, and designing and implementing a new curriculum in economics.

Tradition as Possibility of Change

The stories and enthymemes bring to light the unifying force that captures MSU faculty's hearts and shapes their vision of change. This force is the Soviet tradition. By definition, traditions have a conserving power, preserving knowledge, methods, approaches and practices in organizations. Consisting of rules, norms, and beliefs, traditions also have a pronounced symbolic significance: they serve as mental world maps that organizational members invoke to understand the reality. For example, the enthymemes demonstrate how MSU faculty apply their assumptions of the Soviet system to understand Western methods of teaching and curricular design. When Western methods are found to be predictably different from their Soviet counterparts, they not only stand in competition with old practices but also present a challenge to an entire worldview expressed in the Soviet tradition.

Nevertheless, the institution of Soviet tradition has a potential for change. The concept of routines is useful in understanding this potential. Defined as "complex sets of interlocking behaviors, held in place through common agreement on the relevant roles and expectations" (Feldman, 1989, p. 136), organizational routines are ubiquitous. They contain procedural rules, guide the allocation of authority, and prescribe appropriate courses of action in old and novel situations (March and Olsen, 1989). Feldman and Pentland (2003) point out that along with the ostensive aspect (in the MSU case, the rules about how education should be organized), routines have a performative aspect. In other words, in order to exist at all, routines have to be continuously enacted and performed in the every day life. Indeed, if MSU faculty decided that their Soviet 'world maps' were obsolete, they would no longer interpret the world in terms of Soviet models and practices, and routine behaviors in Soviet-style teaching and curricular design would die out.

It is this performative aspect of routines that contains flexibility and the possibility of change (Feldman and Pentland, 2003). Enacting routines over time, organizational members add their interpretations to them, causing modifications that are subsequently absorbed in the behavior pattern without an overt challenge to the larger worldview. Adoption of written forms of student evaluation is an example of this process. Although written tests and essay exams existed in the Soviet higher education, the emphasis was on oral presentation. MSU prided itself on its students' oratory skills and regarded them as evidence of MSU excellence. The shift toward a Western practice of mid-term tests and end-of-the-term papers was perceived as a rationalized solution to the problems of subjectivity in student evaluations and students' inadequate writing skills. Even the critics who believe that written exams destroy the Soviet oratory tradition accepted the premise of improving student quality control. Routinely prescribed written tests and assignments are now perceived as contributing to the quality of MSU education.

To summarize, the Soviet tradition as a set of routine behaviors, rules, norms, and beliefs not only structures the behavior and worldview of MSU faculty and administration, but also holds potential for change. This change potential is not readily discerned within the discourse on the excellence of the Soviet tradition and its transcendental and immutable value. Uniting the MSU faculty under the banner of institutional excellence and allowing for incremental change, the Soviet tradition plays the role of an invisible hero in the MSU EF stories.

Positive and Negative Rationalization

The reconstructed enthymeme elements reveal two kinds of rationalization themes: positive and negative. Examples of positive rationalization include the use of written examinations and introduction of Bachelor's and Master's degree programs. Both decisions are believed to improve education at the MSU EF. Written tests allegedly remedied subjectivity in evaluations. The decision of the Academic Council to replace the Soviet system of five-year programs with the Western two-tier system signaled progress and development.

The negative rationalization is paradoxical because it ostensibly negates the positive: written examinations are believed to be destructive of the Soviet tradition, and baccalaureate study is often accused of lacking depth. Yet, at the MSU EF the two coexist in competition. This coexistence was observed by Westrum (1990) who studied technological innovations and discovered that organizations can simultaneously propagate two logics: the rhetoric of denial and the rhetoric of affirmation.

Besides rationalizing the inclusion of or resistance to the Western discipline, the MSU EF changes its organizational space and history in order to adapt economics.

Horizontal and Vertical Reorganization: Changes in Spatial Contexts

Internal structural changes. At the start of the MSU EF transition to economics, the existing departments were powerful enough to avoid major reorganization. Having preserved themselves structurally, they re-oriented their activities toward Western economic fields closest to their former Soviet specializations. Since economic fields were broader than what the Faculty structure could fit, more departments were opened to accommodate them. At the same time, economics was decoupled from its Western program structure. Transplanted to the MSU EF, it became a neighbor to business education courses, which in the West are kept separate from programs in economics. In addition to modifying its horizontal structures, the Faculty transformed its vertical organization by eliminating five-year specialist programs and introducing baccalaureate and Master's degrees. This transformation eased the adoption of Western economic programs by re-creating their two-tier structure in the local MSU setting.

Geographic expansion. Expansion of activities over a large geographical area is characteristic of MSU's translation of economics. Collaboration with leading universities abroad ensures that MSU's development of economic fields occurs along the lines accepted by the world academic community. The world community of economists is the reference group that is simultaneously a source of scholarly authority and financial resources. It is not accidental then, that the Faculty has more partners abroad than in the NIS where strong economic programs are still few and the resources are low. The enthymemes demonstrate this value of ties with the West: Western universities are assumed to have the best models of programs, courses, teaching guides and internal departmental changes, and association with them contributes to Russian universities' success and development.

The stories and reconstructed enthymemes also reflect MSU beliefs about institutional size and geographic location. The stories repeatedly contrast MSU to small universities and universities located outside of the two capitals (Moscow and St. Petersburg). Reconstructed enthymemes make explicit the assumption that the large size and central geographical location of a university affect its quality. Furthermore, it is understood that the negative effects of peripheral location are neutralized if the university is of large size. Thus, in MSU's rhetoric, small universities like the Higher School of Economics are inherently inferior to MSU.

Manipulation of Time and Tradition: Changes in Temporal Contexts

In creating a hospitable temporal context for Western economics, the MSU EF had to decide how the new field would fit the University's history and how the University's history could be made to accommodate the new field. To remind the reader, the MSU has at least a two-centuries old tradition of teaching economic sciences. Until the October Revolution of 1917, MSU economic scientists were part of the European scholarly community. Therefore, seventy years of the Soviet rejection of economics as a false science may be viewed as a rupture in the time continuum of the field's development at MSU. From the organizational point of view, this rupture has a negative valence: it casts the University's history as lacking a scholarly tradition, expertise, and reputation. Not to appear 'lacking' the MSU EF had either to mend this rupture or revise its history to show that the rupture did not exist.

Denouncing the Soviet Past: time suspension. Reconnecting to the University's pre-Soviet past is one of the historical revisionist approaches employed at the MSU EF. From this perspective, when MSU economists return to their legitimate roots in the early 20th century and reconstruct economic science from there, seventy years of Soviet political economy becomes a deviation from the course. As a deviation, the Soviet economic science can be judged irrelevant and suspended from the accounts of continuity in the MSU excellence. The reconstructed enthymeme premises and conclusions about the legitimacy of Western economics and illegitimacy of Soviet political economy present examples of this thinking. Respondents talk about returning to 'normal' economic science rather than adopting it anew. Returning to the normal roots implies cutting out the Soviet roots as abnormal and stitching the distant past and the immediate present together.

Transfiguration of tradition. While some stories of change at the MSU EF revise the University history by suspending its Soviet past, other accounts focus on a few strong elements of the Soviet system and interpret change as transfigured tradition. MSU beliefs about the superiority of the Soviet tradition and anticipation of economics by cybernetics have been described earlier. In this logic, the Soviet economic science, albeit imperfect, was indeed a legitimate science. Therefore, in order to make the MSU history receptive of the Western discipline, the Faculty needs not to abolish but to transfigure the existing Soviet tradition by changing research agendas, shifting ideological positions, and adding new elements. This type of modification in the University's temporal context is reflected in the official versions of the MSU EF transition to Western economics.

Whether it suspends the Soviet past or transfigures it, the MSU EF forgets some part of its history, allowing for the absorption of new elements. This selective organizational amnesia smoothes the conflict between old practices and innovations. It may be said, therefore, that MSU is what Cameron (1984) calls a 'Janusian institution': it looks simultaneously to the past and toward the future. By retaining stability associated with the Soviet tradition and developing flexibility, the University adapts Western economics without challenging its core identity.

The next and the last case in the book takes the study to a different geographical location to examine the adaptation of economics by Ural State University in Ekaterinburg.

Chapter Six
Ural State University: A Regional Center of Economic Education

Like Moscow State, Ural State University belongs to the group of classical universities with a wide range of programs in the humanities, the social, natural, and hard sciences. Unlike MSU, it does not have a pre-Soviet history: it was founded three years after the October Revolution of 1917 with the explicit goal to prepare specialists for the Soviet state. Located on the border between Europe and Asia, USU does not have the benefits of Moscow's academic infrastructure and had to establish its own channels of communication with Western scholarly communities. USU is a central university in the Ural Region and therefore influential in the development of economics in the territory outside of Moscow and St. Petersburg.

The structure of the chapter repeats the organization of the previous two chapters. I begin with a case consisting of an account of USU events created primarily from university publications. The official account is followed by an analysis of most frequently told USU stories and an examination of assumptions reconstructed from the stories with the help of the rhetorical analysis. At the end of the chapter, I bring together the findings from the case, stories, and reconstructed enthymemes in an overall analysis of the translation of economics by USU.

BUILDING ECONOMICS ON MATH: THE CASE OF URAL STATE UNIVERSITY

The Soviet Roots

Geographic location. Ural State University is located in the administrative center of Sverdlovsk Region (*oblast*), the city of Ekaterinburg (renamed Sverdlovsk in the Soviet Union and renamed Ekaterinburg again in the

1990s). The Region is known for its fuel industry, ferrous metallurgy, and machine building. Eighty-eight percent of 4.5 million people living in the Region reside in cities (Sevruk, 2002). In the academic year of 2001–2002, there were 174,800 higher education students in the Region, including 153,100 in state institutions and 21,700 in the private sector (Sokolin, 2002).

Founded in the name of Katherine the Great in the 18th century, the city of Ekaterinburg is located approximately a thousand miles from Moscow—not a particularly long distance, considering Russia's territory. With the population of approximately 1.3 million people, Ekaterinburg is the fifth largest city in Russia. The city is also considered to be the fourth science center in the nation: it has the Ural Branch of the Russian Academy of Sciences (UB RAS), 18 RAS research institutes, and more than a hundred industrial research institutes and centers (Sevruk, 2002).

Economic education at USU in the Soviet Union. The University was founded in 1920. Initially, USU consisted of six faculties, preparing agricultural and industrial engineers, teachers, doctors, and a variety of specialists in social sciences. As it grew in size and developed, the Ministry extracted professional faculties from the USU structure and formed them into separate educational institutions, leaving the humanities and social sciences at the University. Created in 1960, the Economic Faculty followed the fate of other professional faculties. In 1967, despite the protests of the professoriate, it was retrieved from the University and reorganized into the Sverdlovsk Institute of National Economy (SINE). The SINE began to train applied economists and collaborate with the Academy of Sciences on local economic projects.

Since Marxist political economy was an essential part of the Soviet curriculum in any discipline, the remaining political economists were not dispersed in the University structure. Rather, they were given a department of their own in the Faculty of Philosophy. Under the charismatic leadership of a distinguished Marxist theorist, the Department of Political Economy quickly earned a good reputation among peer institutions in the country. Together with a dedicated group of colleagues, the Department chair lobbied tirelessly with the USU administration and the Ministry to grant the growing department the status of a faculty. In 1983, after fifteen years of hard work and persuasion, the Department was transformed into the Economic Faculty (USU EF).

As was customary in Soviet universities, the bulk of the economic curriculum was reserved for Marxist theoretical subjects and only a small portion was given to mathematical methods of analysis. At the time, USU had already established a good reputation in physics and applied mathematics research. Math departments enjoyed a greater freedom in choosing research topics: unlike scholarship in political science, their abstract investigations were virtually immune to the resolutions of party congresses.

Cyberneticists at USU. Like in all Soviet universities, the hiring of new faculty at USU was planned by the Ministry. The practice of central planning involved rotation of cadres across regions and republics of the Soviet Union. Upon their graduation, students received what was called a 'distribution' or assignment to a position in an organization anywhere in the country. Familiar with the quality of professional preparation at various universities, employers could request graduates from a particular university or institute. Thus, academically-minded graduates from leading universities tended to be 'distributed' to leading universities.

In 1983, a young economist was assigned to USU from Siberia. Nadezhda Bogolyubova was a graduate in cybernetics at Novosibirsk State University (NSU)—the university that would later supply USU with designers of its first courses in economics. The city of Novosibirsk housed the Siberian branch of the Academy of Sciences and was regarded as the third national science center after Moscow and St. Petersburg. Among economists, NSU was especially well-known for its programs in mathematical analysis of the economy, or as it was called, cybernetics. Hiring cyberneticists from a leading university promised a stronger mathematical component for the program and possibly, a balance of power between Marxist political economists and mathematicians at the Faculty. Together with a graduate from the Moscow State cybernetics program, Bogolyubova would anticipate some elements of Western economic science in her course design long before economics was introduced in USU.

Student Initiative in Curricular Change

Student activism in the time of change. In 1987, the Soviet leader Michail Gorbachev initiated political and economic reforms. Known as *perestroika*, the reforms called for the democratization of political life and greater economic accountability of state enterprises. The spirit and the goals of perestroika resonated with a group of the USU EF students who had become increasingly dissatisfied with the theoretical and ideological nature of their education. These students were active members of so-called 'academic circles' (*nauchnye kruzhki*), peer groups with shared academic or research interests, and had a strong interest in researcher and faculty careers. Eager to improve teaching at the Faculty, they searched for economists who could fill in what they perceived as gaps in their preparation as economists. Some of them, notably, Klara Sabirianova and Sergei Kadochnikov, even traveled to St. Petersburg to persuade academic economists there to come and teach a course at USU.

In the early 1990s, the students began to approach USU faculty and administrators with a proposal to change the existing economic curriculum. While some faculty did not believe that the curriculum needed change, others were sympathetic to the idea. Among those who supported the student activists were Daria Nesterova and Nadezhda Bogolyubova. A graduate of one of the first classes at the SINE, Nesterova had extensive teaching and research experience in economic sciences. In 1990, she started her graduate studies for the Doctor of Sciences Degree at the UB RAS Institute of Economy and was also interested in upgrading economic programs with the latest knowledge in the field. A graduate of the NSU program in cybernetics, Bogolyubova was a faculty member in the Department of Political Economy and therefore had first-hand experience teaching math in an ideologically laden environment. In 1990 she defended her candidate of sciences degree at the highly respected Moscow Financial Institute. The fact that in 1991 Bogolyubova became Vice Dean for Academic Affairs and Nesterova was appointed Acting Dean helped students to advance their cause of curricular reform.

Student and faculty collaboration. With active participation of Nesterova and Bogolyubova, a group of faculty formed a curriculum committee at the Academic Council and invited the student activists to take part in the meetings. In the meantime, the students also formed a curricular group, where they discussed what economic education should look like with regard to practical applications to the economy. The results of the discussions were then formed into proposals and presented at the meetings of the Academic Council. Sabirianova, who graduated in 1989 and immediately began her graduate studies at the UB RAS Institute of Economy, continued to take an active part in the discussions. Kadochnikov, who upon graduation in 1991 followed Sabirianova's route, also stayed involved.

The students read through everything they could find about economic education abroad. However, information on Western program design was limited. The students had to rely on common sense and their observations of the changing environment in developing curricular proposals for the USU EF. They wanted more applied courses, less political economy, and opportunities for interdisciplinary studies. The activism of the group antagonized some faculty members, who believed it was inappropriate to involve students in curricular design and who objected to the substance of the proposed curricular changes. Years later, reflecting on the work of the student group during perestroika, one of its members recalled a sense of exhilaration and responsibility brought about by the subversion of the Soviet canon: "It was revolutionary, truly revolutionary. We were young and romantic . . . The time was romantic."

The student initiatives of the early 1990s coincided in time with a series of hires that proved transformational for the USU EF. A group of Siberian graduates of the NSU cybernetics program were 'distributed' to teach at USU. As experts in mathematical analyses of economic processes, they were closest in their training to Western math-intensive economics. Therefore, they were assigned to design courses in micro, macroeconomics, and econometrics. In the fall of 1990, when the incoming freshman class saw their first schedules, Marxist-Leninist Philosophy was still on the top of their course list. A year later, the freshman course list was opened by Foundations of Market Economy/ Economics. Although political economy stayed in the program, albeit in a reduced form, Marxism-Leninism was nowhere to be seen from then on.

However, the curricular change at USU progressed slowly. The Ministry controlled USU organization and the National Standards of Education formed a formidable barrier to changing the structure and content of education. The private sector offered greater flexibility in institutional forms and a better money making opportunity. Thus, with an interdisciplinary group of colleagues, Nesterova and Bogolyubova participated in the creation of the Ural Institute of Economics, Law, and Management (UIELM), which they joined in 1992 at a fraction of faculty appointment, continuing to teach at USU. The Institute was quick to respond to the demand for economists with the knowledge of market economy and the expertise in business administration. In the years to come, first as Vice Rector and then as Rector of the Institute, Nesterova would invite more of her USU colleagues and graduate students for a joint appointment at the UIELM. In 1993, at USU Nesterova was appointed Dean of the Economic Faculty.

Travel Abroad and International Exchange

In the early 1990s, USU graduate students and faculty began to travel abroad. Coming back from those first exchanges, they applied what they learned in their courses, upgrading the old material with new knowledge. Looking back at the first infusions of economics in the existing curriculum, a participant of the first exchanges observed, "Reflecting on those first attempts now, I understand that what we got as a result was neither Soviet nor Western economics, but at least it was something, it was a progressive movement away from the old."

It was not until 1994 that the curriculum change acquired a more directed character. That year, Nesterova traveled to Munchen Technical

University in Germany as a visiting professor, Sabirianova went to the University of Kentucky College of Business and Economics as a visiting scholar, and Kadochnikov earned a Master's Degree in Economics from Constance University in Germany. Having completed their programs, Sabirianova assumed the position of Associate Dean for International Affairs at the USU EF, while Kadochnikov began to teach there in the position of Assistant Professor. Since that time, the Faculty have established regular student and faculty exchanges with the University of Gent, Belgium, SERGE in Prague, the Czech Republic, and several German universities.

Furthermore, the year of 1994 marked the beginning of successful grant writing. In the period from 1995 to 1998, Nesterova and her colleagues received three European Commission Tempus-Tacis grants for research and improvement of international exchange of economists, a grant from the World Bank for an electronic textbook, two research grants from Russian foundations and a grant from the Soros Foundation.

Undergraduate and Graduate Curricular Development

The Faculty opened a Bachelor's program in 1993. Having decided to introduce Western-style baccalaureate and master's programs, the Faculty nevertheless left the Soviet five-year programs intact. As the employers began to recognize Bachelor's and Master's degrees, the five-year specialist programs were re-conceptualized as in-depth preparation for students planning a teaching career or intending to pursue a candidate of sciences degree.

With a few foreign exchanges and mathematical economists on the Faculty, designing introductory courses in micro and macroeconomics was accomplished rather quickly. Furthermore, in 1995 upon her return from Kentucky, Sabirianova proposed to replace the practice of oral examinations with the U.S. system of mid-term tests and end-of-the-term written assignments. The innovation was adopted first by the departments teaching economic theory, then by the rest of the faculty.

Designing specialization courses for the senior year of the baccalaureate and for the master's program turned out to be more challenging. With their knowledge of foreign languages, only a handful of faculty could participate in exchanges with Western universities or consult with Western peers in writing. Furthermore, in the absence of intermediate and advanced literature in economic fields, the USU EF faculty could not learn them on their own. In short, the faculty needed retraining and systematic consultations in Russian. Such opportunity came along in 1999 in the form of the Soros Foundation's Megaproject on Development of Education in Russia.

Table 6.1. USU EF Departments and Corresponding Economic Fields

Department	Economic Field
Not a separate department	A. General Economics & Teaching
Economic Theory & World Economy	B. Schools of Economic Thought & Methodology
Economic Modeling & Informatics	C. Mathematical & Quantitative Methods
Economic History & International Economics	D. Microeconomics
	E. Macroeconomics & Monetary Economics
	F. International Economics
	G. Financial Economics
	H. Public Economics
	I. Health, Education, & Welfare
	J. Labor & Demographic Economics
Economics & Law	K. Law & Economics
Not a separate department	L. Industrial Organization
Theory & Practice of Management; Advertising; Public Relations	M. Business Administration & Business Economics; Marketing; Accounting
(see Economic History & International Economics)	N. Economic History
Not a separate department	O. Economic Development, Technological Change, & Growth
Organizational Economic Systems	P. Economic Systems
Not a separate department	Q. Agricultural & Natural Resource Economics
	R. Urban, Rural, & Regional Economics
	Z. Other Special Topics

Megaproject on the Development of Education in Russia

Sponsored by the Soros Foundation's Open Society Institute, the project aimed at strengthening Russian departments in the humanities and social sciences. In the USU case, it partnered the Department of Economic History and International Economics with the New School of Economics (NSE) in

Moscow for a series of exchanges, seminars, and summer schools. Organized and run as a joint Russian-American Master's granting institution, the NSE is a small elite school with a world-wide reputation in economic theory, most notably, economics of transition. With the flexible system of faculty appointments and generous salaries, the NSE invites leading American, European, and Russian professors to teach at the School. This is how the USU EF faculty members studying at the NSE met professors from Moscow State and the Higher School of Economics who became their academic advisors and research collaborators.

As a result of collaboration with the NSE, the Department created advanced level courses in several economic fields. With some overlap in their specializations, the USU EF departments now represent all areas of undergraduate and Master's economic curricula as they are known in the West[1] (see Table 6.1).

Organizational Restructuring and Growth

Internal structural changes. The introduction of new economic fields led to renaming and reorganizing the existing departments. In 1995, the oldest USU EF Department of Political Economy became the Department of Economic History and International Economics (DEHIE). The popular demand for managers led to the addition of courses in marketing and management. As courses in professional preparation, they were less rigorous than theoretical courses in economics, creating inconsistencies in student workload and evaluation. After a period of uncomfortable coexistence, economics and management separated and the faculty members teaching management formed a department of their own. Departments of Public Relations and Advertising were added to the USU management programs a couple of years later.

Departments responsible for programs in economics expanded in size, but did not multiply. In 1999, when the DEHIE began its long-term partnership with the New School of Economics, there were about three dozen full-time and adjunct faculty members at the USU EF. Although the DEHIE was one of the largest in size, it was small enough to operate as a single unit.

The Russian-American Institute. In 2000 Sabirianova defended her PhD at the University of Kentucky and was hired as Assistant Professor at the William Davidson Institute (WDI) at the University of Michigan Business School, Ann Arbor. This event signified a new turn in the USU EF development. In the course of the following years, USU faculty members traveled to Ann Arbor to do research and take courses at the WDI. In the winter of 2001, Nesterova visited Sabirianova in the U.S. to meet the WDI faculty and administrators and to discuss a project of creating a Russian-American consulting center in economics on the USU premises. Two years later, this idea materialized as the Russian American Institute of Economics and Business (RAIEB). Founded as a center for applied economics and business, the RAIEB admitted its first students in the fall of 2004.

Epilogue

By 2004 the USU EF became to be recognized as one of the country's leading centers of economics. With a small and motivated collective of academic economists, the USU EF was successful in attracting large and small grants for curricular development and research. In 2002, the USU EF commenced a second long-term partnership project with the NSE aimed at strengthening another unit: the Department of Economic Theory and World Economy. The Faculty hosts international and regional conferences and invites faculty members from regional universities to the joint USU-NSE summer schools.

As a Faculty of the classical university, the USU EF is a member of the Teaching and Methodological Association (UMO in Russian abbreviation) for Classical Universities in economics. Housed at Moscow State University, UMO meetings are valuable opportunities for resource and information-starved regional professors to learn about the latest innovations at MSU. MSU was the first virtually in everything: converting to baccalaureate and Master's programs, changing curricula, establishing regular exchange programs, etc. Regional universities could only hope to accomplish as much in the future. Imagine her surprise when once during a much anticipated MSU report on curricular change, Nesterova realized that there was nothing new in what she was hearing. Everything that Moscow State did the USU EF had done years before. The memorable meeting occurred in the mid-1990s, but the epiphany has stayed with her since: "I realized that we are no less than MSU and that we are going the right way in what we are doing here. And we can accomplish so much more . . ."

USU STORIES AND ASSUMPTIONS: THE WORLD MADE BETTER BY MATH

The case describes the introduction of economics in the USU EF as a product of student activism and faculty expertise in mathematics. It shows how the USU EF capitalizes on its Soviet legacy of cutting edge research in mathematics and strives to play an active role internationally. Thus, like MSU,

USU blends the elements of the old and new systems together. The USU stories and reconstructed enthymemes illuminate the beliefs and taken-for-granted knowledge that guide this blending of the Soviet and Western practices by USU faculty, administrators, and graduates.

Ninety-nine stories were derived from nine interviews with the administrators, faculty, and graduates of Ural State University. Ten stories were accounts of personal life and were discarded as irrelevant to the study. The remaining 89 stories presented accounts of the events that happened at the USU EF before and after the USU introduced economics. The stories were examined for common themes and coded by topic. The results of the coding are presented in Appendix C. After identifying and rebuilding enthymemes from 89 USU stories, 298 implied premises and conclusions were reconstructed. Twenty-seven of 298 enthymeme sentences referred to persons and were excluded from the analysis. The remaining 271 enthymeme premises and conclusions were examined for common themes and coded. The enthymeme coding results for USU are presented in Appendix F.

The largest group of stories consisted of recollections on three interconnected topics: the beginning of the transition to Western-style economics (n=9), the role of students in initiating this change (n=7), and the role of Siberian professors of mathematics in this trasition (n=5). The accounts below illustrate these transition stories (total n=21). In the first one, the faculty member recalls the time when cyberneticists were invited to make changes in the curriculum. His/her choice of the word *perestroika* is notable because it typically refers to Russian political and economic reforms of the late 1980s and early 1990s. By calling the changes at the USU EF perestroika, the faculty member underscores their significance for the University:

> As I heard, the perestoika began in 1992. It was the year when graduates of Novosibirk State University came to the Faculty. There were four or five of them. Novosibirsk State is famous for its preparation—they have always been known for it—their economic theory, there has always been a very strong math component. Their specialization was mathematical cybernetics. So they found themselves in the *mainstream* easily [English term in respondent's narrative]. And I don't know whose idea it was to change the academic plan—it was probably [student name withdrawn] but as far as I understand, they [cyberneticists] were charged with the task to design new courses and they did it.

In the second story, a former student activist remembers the beginning of the curricular change at the USU EF. He/she gives an evaluative assessment of Soviet economic education (it had "abnormal" foundations) and romanticizes the past:

> The time was indeed transitional and there was an interest on the side of the faculty members to give normal foundations of theoretical economics in a contemporary sense. There was undoubtedly an interest on the side of students for many reasons—undoubtedly, because of their desire to acquire modern professional education, and because of the young blood, the hunger for revolution and innovation. The time was romantic.

Although the two accounts of the transition describe the events that happened some twenty years after the Faculty was established, they have features of a foundation saga. The main heroes—either Siberian mathematicians or idealistic hot-blooded students hungry for revolution, or both—overcome the conservatism of the ideologically charged USU EF and after struggle and deprivation, manage to accomplish the unthinkable: set the fossilized Soviet university in motion for change. In the case of the mathematicians, the change is re-writing the curriculum to include economics. In the case of the students, it is making the economic program relevant to contemporary economic practices and ridding the curriculum of Marxist ideology.

The ultimate outcomes of the heroes' efforts are unimportant: the students' ideas were implemented only partially, and the first courses in economics had to be subsequently re-designed. What is important, however, is what is remembered: the Siberian mathematicians and the group of student activists were the catalysts of change that led to the present-day achievements of the Faculty. Therefore, in the organizational memory, the first reformers of the curriculum are preserved with fondness and affective exaggeration. They are a source of pride and they personify the values that the Faculty espouses. The stories also tacitly express the value of math as a foundation of the USU EF economics program. In this sense, the USU transition stories function as organizational sagas (Clark, 1972), uniting the faculty members through a common history and reinforcing their organizational identity.

The examination of enthymemes reconstructed from the USU stories reveals that USU respondents indeed take it for granted that student interests should be taken into account in curricular design. Yet the enthymeme analysis also shows that student involvement in curricular decisions is not regarded as a standard practice at the University. To the dissatisfaction of faculty, students are believed to prefer practice-oriented courses rather than theory and to be less actively involved in research today than they were in the Soviet Union. Thus, student interest in curricular development is welcomed with cautiousness.

In the USU narratives, the Soviet Union invokes several nostalgic memories containing a number of positive assumptions about the Soviet system of education: it is believed that scientists in Soviet universities had a collegial culture and the State took good care of academics. Moreover, it is presumed that in the Soviet Union mathematicians were little affected by ideology, had a better financial position than they have now, and kept abreast of contemporary trends in world economics unlike their colleagues in political economy who were supposed to be isolated from the international community by the Soviet ideology. Since mathematics is understood to be an apolitical science and cybernetics is believed to be close to economics, it is taken for granted that cyberneticists learned the Western discipline readily and didn't have to change what they taught as the country transitioned from a planned to a market economy. At the same time, economic education in the Soviet Union in general is viewed as inadequate, and the development of Soviet mathematics is believed to be slowed down by the scarcity of available foreign literature in their field. The elimination of Marxist political economy from the university curricula in the 1990s is seen as a sign of progress.

The theme of the importance of mathematics cuts across many USU narratives and occupies a prominent place in the discussion of program quality. Like their peers at HSE and MSU, USU respondents take it for granted that in order to design new programs in economics, one would need to know the discipline, have an idea about the goals of the program, and look at Western models of education. However, unlike the other two schools in the study, USU views mathematics not only as an essential part of a program in economics, but also as a measure of the program quality. As the enthymeme analysis shows, knowledge of math is understood as key to learning economics and designing programs of study. It is presumed that a strong math component is an indicator of a good program, that adding econometrics to a curriculum signifies its improvement, and using math models in course design makes it more advanced.

Another large group of USU stories account for the adaptation of the Western disciplinary content and teaching methods to the Russian context (n=12). The story below illustrates the process of creating new economic textbooks by Russian universities.

> Adaptation [of textbooks] went fast. You see, the books that are translated are mainly those books that were extremely popular in the West, and if they are popular, it means that they are not of a very high level: "popular" means "for many people" and if something is for many people, it isn't of high level. At the university level, one should set higher requirements. So articles or chapters were translated quickly and then compiled into readers. This [practice] is also common at MSU. When

they create programs, they do not just translate Western books but they also adapt them in some way, take some materials from Russian articles and this is how their textbooks appear. But when they [the books] appear, they are already dated for our universities.

The story explains how foreign works get translated and compiled in textbooks by Russian universities, and establishes a distinction between basic popular texts and advanced books with a clear preference for the latter. Notably, the example the author of the story uses to illustrate the process of adaptation is based on the practices of Moscow State University that for years has been regarded as a model for emulation by regional universities. Adaptation is defined in the excerpt as translation and modification (MSU doesn't "just translate Western books but they also adapt them in some way"). The story suggests that the subject of economic analysis in Russia—the country's economy—is changing rapidly: by the time textbooks come out of the printing press, their content may already be outdated.

The reference to Moscow State in the story is emblematic of the USU EF process of establishing their organizational identity as a leading economic faculty in the country. Defining themselves in relation to best schools, the USU EF demonstrates that it is itself part of that group of best schools. The reconstructed enthymeme elements illustrate how USU respondents perceive their University in relation to leading Russian and U.S. universities and where they place themselves in the hierarchy of institutional quality. Although USU administrators, faculty, and graduates assume the excellence of MSU programs, they believe that the USU program in economics is designed as well as that at MSU. Speaking of their partner institutions, the respondents implicitly acknowledge the superiority of the New School of Economics and the University of Michigan. At the same time, the fact that USU collaborates with famous scholars at these universities is seen as an indicator of institutional quality. Similarly, regular student exchanges between USU and Western universities as well as personal interactions between USU faculty and their Western peers are believed to be signs of the USU EF prestige and its integration in the world scholarly community.

Adapting the Western discipline to fit the Russian context may be problematic not only because of the short life span new textbooks enjoy before they become outdated, as suggested by the story above. The rhetorical analysis of the USU stories on the same topic uncovers tacit understandings and assumptions about competing values of Western and Soviet practices. Although the West is presumed to be a source of educational models, not all of them are perceived favorably. Compared to the Soviet five-year programs, Bachelor's and Master's programs are believed to be inferior in the quality of education they provide. By contrast, the Soviet system of specialized senior seminars in the areas of student interest is seen as superior to Master's specialization. Other Western practices are perceived positively. It is assumed that written forms of evaluation widely used in the West are more suitable to courses in economic theory than the Soviet practice of end-of-the-term oral examinations.

The tension between Western and Soviet economic traditions is also reflected in USU discussions about generational gap of the faculty and their ability to teach and do research in economics. USU administrators, faculty, and graduates take it for granted that research is important at USU and that the quality of a department is measured by the number of grants it acquires. Similar to their HSE and MSU colleagues, USU respondents perceive age as a predictor of the faculty member's ability to learn new disciplines, assume that old faculty are unlikely to be capable of learning and teaching economics, and believe that the willingness to learn and study regularly is an essential characteristic of good faculty. Unlike their Moscow peers, in their narratives USU respondents presume that the choice of Western vs. Russian research projects in economics also depends on the age of the faculty member. Young faculty members are believed to be more interested in international projects than their senior colleagues. It is also assumed that research for Russian granting agencies is more useful for Russia than research for Western granting agencies.

Another facet of the adaptation of economics to the Russian context is described in USU narratives as the problem of balancing theory and application. Like many other Russian universities, when USU faculty began to build a program in economics in the early 1990s, they did not make distinction between economic and business education, combining both strands of knowledge in one program. Several years later, perceived as more theoretical, economics was separated from its more applied cousin of business administration. However, the disagreement about the proportion of theory and practice in the economic program persisted. The rhetorical analysis of USU stories on the topic reflects the complexity of this problem. On the one hand, it is taken for granted that programs should not mix economic theory with applied disciplines such as management, accounting, and auditing. The blending of the two is expected to decrease the quality of theoretical preparation because theoretical knowledge is believed to be superior to professional education. On the other hand, it is assumed that good courses consist of theoretical lectures and laboratory practice and that they show the relevance of the discipline to real life. Since math is considered to be the main strength of the USU EF, it is expected that a good math department should offer many practice-oriented math courses and good mathematicians should demonstrate to their students how to apply abstract math models in practice.

Thus, the characteristic feature of the USU stories and enthymemes is an abundance of references to mathematics. Math and programs in math are believed to be a foundation of economics, a bridge between the Soviet and Western economic sciences, a stabilizing force in USU organizational changes, and a sign of institutional quality. Furthermore, mathematics is assumed to be apolitical and timeless: no ideology can affect it and it exists in all political regimes, Soviet or capitalist. However, this belief in math's transcendental nature is contradictory to expectations regarding its applicability to practice. Good mathematicians are required to show how to apply abstract models to the real world, which is, by definition, mutable.

USU CASE ANALYSIS

The USU case is a case of an anticipated transition to Western economics and self-education in economic curricular development. Unlike HSE and MSU, Ural State does not have the advantage of a central location with its access to resources and information. In their own accounts, when the faculty at the USU EF began to introduce alterations in academic programs, they were isolated from the Western academic community. The initial changes were based not on the knowledge of what economics was but on what faculty and students *believed* it was. The belief in the closeness of cybernetics and economics added confidence to their endeavors. Most importantly, the student initiative taken up by the faculty gave an impetus for the transformations to follow.

Rationalization of Transformation

The transition sagas present the changes in the Faculty as a constant effort to improve teaching methods and content in economics. For example, one of Sabirianova's many contributions to the development of economics at the USU is written evaluations. Having visited universities in the U.S., she persuaded her colleagues to adopt a Western practice of standardized tests and written examinations as more suitable for evaluating the students' knowledge of economic theory. Although this practice was more labor intensive, the faculty members began voluntarily to assign more written tests because they believed them to be better evaluation instruments than

Soviet end-of-the-term oral exams. Thus, the adoption of a new practice was understood and accepted by the faculty members as rationalized improvement.

Another example of rationalized improvement is the USU EF collaborative projects with the New School of Economics. As the reconstructed enthymemes elements show, the NSE is assumed to have the latest knowledge in the field. Therefore, a partnership with the NSE imparts excellence to the USU EF economics curriculum. Mathematics supplies yet another string of rationalization discourse at the USU. As the enthymemes demonstrate, in the tacit understanding of USU faculty, as a pure science, math is devoid of irrationality in contrast to other disciplines in the Soviet curriculum that may be infused with ideology. Therefore, transitioning to math-intensive economics signals strengthening of the rational component of economic education and improves the quality of the program. In addition to creating rationalized accounts of innovation adoption, the USU EF modifies the University organizational context and history in order to smooth the transition to the Western discipline.

Intensive Internal Development and Expanding Networks: Changes in Spatial Contexts

Intensive vs. extensive development. Most of the departmental reorganizations at the USU EF occurred as a consequence of discipline boundary setting. As the number of applied business education courses grew, the faculty members found themselves divided by the different philosophies, goals, methods, and content of economics and management specializations. Thus, new departments were formed on the foundations of restructured old ones.

With a small collective of faculty members who designed and taught courses in economics, the USU EF took an intensive rather than extensive approach to development. In other words, instead of creating more departments to accommodate different fields of economic knowledge, the Faculty intensified the workload in the existing units. The partnership projects with the NSE illustrate this trend for intensive development. First, the Department of Economic History and International Economics professors developed expertise in a wide range of economic fields, then the USU EF shifted resources in order to upgrade the Department of Economic Theory and World Economy.

Symbolic geographic expansion. As the reconstructed enthymemes suggest, USU faculty place high value on international student exchanges and personal scholarly interactions with their Western colleagues. However, the USU geographic location places constraints on its international interactions: few foreign faculty travel to the Ural Region, preferring the well-established academic infrastructures in Moscow and St. Petersburg.

Nevertheless, the USU EF found ways to connect to the world academic community. In doing so, the Faculty followed at least two routes. First, through a long-term partnership project with the New School of Economics, it became part of networks of leading economists in Europe and in Russia. As students at the NSE programs and summer schools, the USU faculty observed the NSE's organization and daily operation. Moreover, since their teachers at the NSE were professors from Moscow State and the Higher School of Economics, the USU faculty formed an impression about other Moscow universities. Collaborative research projects with NSE professors strengthened the USU EF reputation as a research center in the Ural Region and added to the content of its programs.

The second route to international academia was paved by USU EF graduates traveling abroad for study and work. Sabirianova's efforts to put the USU EF on the map of the U.S. academic community were especially fruitful. Not only did her initiatives give the USU faculty an opportunity to do research together with American colleagues, but they also led to establishing the Russian-American Institute. Designed specifically as a combination of Russian and American organizational models, the Institute is an attempt to create an organized space that is more conducive to the development of economics than the existing structures at the Faculty.

Unlike MSU and HSE that expanded geographically by establishing joint programs with universities abroad and opening branches in Russia, the USU EF geographic expansion is more symbolic than material. Nevertheless, USU's international collaborations serve similar purposes: they increase the production of economic knowledge by the Faculty, improve its curriculum, and legitimize the USU faculty members' interpretation of economics.

Selective Interpretation of Tradition: Changes in Temporal Contexts

Unlike Moscow State University, USU does not have a pre-Soviet history of teaching in economic sciences. Founded soon after the Revolution of 1917, Ural State is a Soviet university in its history and design. Therefore, the USU EF cannot suspend the seventy-year period as having no bearing on its scholarly tradition and reconnect to a non-Soviet past. It cannot graft itself on the traditions of Western universities either: its place within the overall University structure would not permit such autonomy. In these circumstances, reinterpreting and transfiguring the Soviet tradition seems to be the only viable solution to creating a temporal context for the Western discipline.

In the MSU stories, the Soviet academic tradition is often described as a monolithic institution consisting of privileged academics, fundamental research, in-depth preparation in political theory and math, and a culture of critical thinking. The USU stories and enthymemes draw a different picture. In revising their history, the USU faculty members adopt a more narrow focus and interpret the Soviet tradition at USU as excellence in mathematical preparation. Cybernetics becomes a precursor of economics, or as a USU professor put it, cybernetics was "latent economics" that in time blossomed into its Western form. In this logic, the curricular changes started by student activists together with a small group of faculty represent not an innovation but an actualization of the latent ideas that had existed in the Soviet university all along. Thus, USU's Soviet history is reconciled to its present day reality and reinterpreted as favorable to the development of economics.

This chapter concludes the presentation of the cases of Russian universities introducing and adapting economics. The next chapter brings the three cases together for an integrative analysis and discussion of intercultural travels of academic fields.

Chapter Seven
Integrative Analysis and Discussion of Intercultural Travels of Academic Fields

The purpose of this chapter is two-fold. First, the integrative analysis of the cases responds to three research questions formulated at the beginning of the inquiry. Namely, what changes occurred in the structure of economics as an academic field when it was adapted to the Russian context? What material and symbolic organizational processes occurred inside universities adapting economics, and who were the main stakeholders of change? What actors in the external environment did the universities engage in the process of adapting economics and how? Answers to these questions combine individual experiences of the universities in the study to create a larger picture of the importation and adaptation of the Western academic field in Russian higher education. Second, the discussion addresses the main question of the study: how does the adaptation of economics by Russian universities add to the understanding of the travel of academic fields across national and cultural borders?

In the first part of the chapter, Integrative Analysis, I follow the Latourian conceptualization of scientific fields presented earlier in the book (see Figure 2.1) and examine each component in the network of economics separately: the phenomena studied by economics and new economic theories; the structure of the disciplinary content (division of economics content into branches); universities and academic communities; actors in the government, political, social and economic spheres; and public opinion. In the analyses of phenomena studied by economics and new economic theories generated in the Russian context, I draw primarily on social studies of science ideas about the social construction of knowledge. My discussion of modifications in the structure of the disciplinary content is based on the concept of translation developed jointly by social studies of science scholars and institutionalists in organization studies. The institutionalist concepts of isomorphism and legitimacy are central to my analyses of universities and academic communities. Similarly, I discuss non-academic political, economic, and social actors, and public opinion in terms of legitimacy concerns of the universities adapting economics.

The examinations of the disciplinary structure and its focus of study (market) provide answers to the first of the three research questions. The analysis of universities explicates material and symbolic transformations in the higher education institutions adapting economics and describes stakeholders of change, responding to the second question of this inquiry. Finally, the third research question—what actors in the external environment the universities engaged in the process of adapting economics and how—is addressed in the analyses of academic and non-academic actors in university environments and public opinion.

In the second part of the chapter, Discussion of Intercultural Travels of Academic Fields, I explore three topics: translators and the process of translation; economics as a macro-actor; and issues of organizational identity. The purpose of this discussion is to use the case of economics in Russia to probe larger issues of intercultural travel of academic fields within the given theoretical framework.

INTEGRATIVE ANALYSIS

The Russian Market Economy as a Focus of Study

In his essays on science studies, Latour (1999) proposes to begin investigations of scientific fields by examining the world that they study. He observes that as sciences describe, analyze, and classify phenomena of nature and society, the phenomena are abstracted from their contexts and become part of the scientific field in the form of samples and artifacts, which are subsequently used in the production of knowledge. Moreover, in order to study the world, scientists develop instruments, surveys, and theoretical formulae, which also become part of the scientific field and are employed to generate new data and facts. Thus, explains Latour (1999), along with scientists, the non-human world of artifacts and instruments participates in the production of scientific knowledge. Therefore, he claims, the world surrounding scientific fields should be analyzed together with or even before the analysis of the scientific content. Latour's observations are pertinent to the present discussion: the Russian market economy is not only a context of economics but also its focus of study, a nonhuman world of data and artifacts.

In Western nations where modern economic theories have developed over the past century, economics is understood to include the study of capitalist market economies and the relations of production and distribution of goods. In Russia, the object of study has been less clearly defined. In the early 1990s, there was no capitalist market in Russia. Contrary to the prognoses of Russian economists, the 1990–1991 economic reforms failed miserably, as did the rouble several times afterwards, and the analysts bemoaned the unruliness of the so-called transition that defied existing formulae and definitions (Rutland, 1999). Therefore, in the early days of its presence in Russian universities, economics was a visitor from the future. Scholarly collaborations between Russian universities and the leading schools of economics in Western Europe and the U.S. became time travels where the Russian scholars could learn about the desirable capitalist future for their country.

In these circumstances, the task of Russian universities was challenging: they could re-create the proper object of study locally or change the content structure of economics to give space for a theory of the emerging market economy. Russian universities did both. The economics of transition (or transitional economics) exemplifies the interconnectedness of the two processes.

First taken up by the New School of Economics, transitional economics studies the conversion of post-Soviet planned economies to the market. Soon after its conception, transitional economics became a legitimate field of expertise for Russian economists. Faculty members at the Higher School of Economics and Moscow State University began to develop the area further, applying theories to research and teaching them to their students. After several semesters at the New School of Economics, Ural State's faculty also became engaged in teaching and research in transitional economics.

With the help of the new conceptual and methodological apparatus, the unruly Russian economy was subjected to analytical techniques that explained its crises and predicted its behavior. Probed, measured, and charted, that vast expanse of the national economy was then re-created in the image of understandable capitalist markets and as such became part of the discourse of Kremlin policy makers, Duma[1] legislators, entrepreneurs, industrialists and common people. If in 1991 people wrote letters to newspapers requesting explanations of market terminology (Argumenti i Fakti, 1991), by the mid-1990s the Russians knew that what was happening with the national economy was called transitioning to a market economy. Thus, transitional economics in Russia was a benefactor and beneficiary of its participation in the creation of a market. As an analytical framework, transitional economics is also a scientific artifact.

The Russian Market Economy as Context

Translation of economics into the language. The structure of economics as an academic field went through several permutations. In the early years of its development in Russia, academics had limited sources of information about what the Western branches of the discipline were like. For decades, the undergraduate textbook of Samuelson translated and abridged in the Soviet Union had been the primary, if not the only, original source of Western economic theory. In the early 1990s, a translation of McConnell and Brue came into print (Ofer & Polterovich, 2000). The translation was done by non-economists and was so incomprehensible that reading it, economists had to interpret it again into the language of economics.

What was the proper terminology of economics was also little known. Some of the standard Western terms could not be translated linguistically, rather they had to be matched with the existing analogues in the Russian economic vocabulary. For example, the Western field of public finance is not immediately recognizable under the Russian term of economics of the public sector (*ekonomika obshchestvennogo sektora*). Similarly, the term 'industrial organizations' is not translated literally, although the language permits it, but is interpreted in the existing terms of economics of industrial markets (*ekonomika otraslevyh rynkov*). Given the complexity of translation, the NSE's solution was both ingenious and effective: the school offered its entire curriculum in English.

Translation of economics into the structure. When Russian universities began to introduce Western economics, they had to fit the discipline into their organizational structure. The fitting showed gaps and discrepancies between the two. The size of the Western economic science with its numerous branches was only part of the problem. As the cases demonstrate, the universities stretched their organizational structure by adding departments to accommodate new economic fields. Transforming the Soviet understanding of the structure of economic science was another matter.

In the Soviet Union, preparation of economists included coursework in accounting and auditing and economic programs contained a mix of theoretical and applied subjects. When economics was imported by Russian universities, it was decoupled from its existing structure where the division between theoretical and applied professional knowledge was stricter. A neighbor first to accounting then to marketing and management, economics in Russian universities had to withstand assaults on its disciplinary boundaries. The departmental reshuffling at Ural State University illustrates this process. At first, when the USU EF professors enthusiastically adopted and adapted individual market-oriented courses, it did not matter that management and macroeconomics were housed at the same department. As the number of new courses increased, the faculty members had to ask themselves if they were building the right discipline. As departments of the Economic Faculty, they were supposed to be advancing economic theory, yet half of the professors were engaged in business education. Moreover, a large group of faculty conflated the two. As the case shows, economic theory at USU was eventually expelled from management, which formed a separate department within the USU EF structure.

As a new university, the Higher School of Economics did not have to establish boundaries for economics. It simply reproduced the structure of Western programs in economics and accepted it as a definition of the disciplinary field. However, the School was not immune to the requirements of the employment market that expected economists to be versed in accounting and other professional subjects. Thus today, even with more clearly defined boundaries of economics, HSE, MSU, and USU supplement it with components of business education in their programs.

Soviet tradition vs. Western orientation. While among the three universities in the study there is a consensus about what should be included in economics programs, there are differences in the opinion about how it should be taught. Although individual teaching methods have little if no effect on the structure of economic science, the discussion about them is emblematic of larger political processes shaping the development of higher education in Russia. These processes also have implications for economics.

MSU and HSE represent two schools of thought on teaching economics. HSE is modeled after a Western university, while MSU is a Soviet model par excellence. Both institutions have a similar program organization (Bachelor's and Master's Degrees) and content structure, and both conduct advanced research in economics. As the stories and enthymemes suggest, the difference lies in the philosophy of education. MSU professors emphasize the Soviet tradition: cultivation of critical thinking, in-depth theoretical preparation, students' excellent oratory skills, and the role of the teacher as a transmitter of knowledge. HSE is regarded as a follower of Western academic traditions with an emphasis on independent learning and critical thinking skills, with sound theoretical preparation in the field, written tests and papers as a method of student evaluation, and democratic interactions between professors and students.

Upon examination of the two sets of characteristics, it becomes clear that the two universities do not represent polar opposites. Furthermore, there is strong factual evidence that today the MSU EF uses predominantly written forms of evaluation, despite some faculty members' negative opinions about them. The faculties of the two universities are not antipodes of each other either, and professors from Moscow State often have part time appointments at HSE.

Nevertheless, in the public discourse MSU and HSE are assumed to be dichotomous. The perception of the two universities as opposites is reinforced by the long lasting confrontation between HSE Rector Kuzminov and MSU Rector Sadovnichii. Their political conflict about the course of educational reforms divided the Russian academic community, labeling the camps as pro-Western and pro-Russian respectively (e.g., Kachurovskaya & Taratuta, 2004). Couching the discussion in terms of a pro-Western vs. pro-Russian choice invokes two centuries of Russian debates between westernizers and slavophiles and therefore is infused with nationalist ideologies. Calling Kuzminov a Harvard joker and insinuating that he sold out to Western academia is an extreme example of these debates (e.g., Komarov, 2002).

Thus, economics in Russia develops in a politically charged environment that either validates or repudiates its Western roots. Furthermore, MSU and HSE disciplinary positions reflect two sources of the discipline's legitimacy in Russia: the old Soviet academia and the Western academic community.

Universities

Sources of faculty authority in innovation. Introducing economics in their departments and faculties for the first time, the academics had to make sure that their innovation was accepted by the local community. Faculty members and administrators had to be convinced that contrary to the Soviet stance, economics was indeed a legitimate and useful science. Researchers had to be persuaded of the validity of its methods. Students had to be assured that it was ultimately more applicable to the Russian economy than Soviet programs and that they would find employment upon graduation. With this amount of convincing to do, the introducers of the innovation had to have a strong authority base. The cases, stories, and enthymemes suggest at least two powerful sources of authority: academic pedigree and specialization in mathematics.

Three types of academic preparation feature prominently in the biographies of the introducers of Western economics. These include a degree from or working experience at Moscow State University, a degree in cybernetics, and an affiliation with the Russian Academy of Sciences. Both Kuzminov and Yasin taught at MSU before they founded HSE. Kuzminov was also a MSU graduate. Both had an affiliation with RAS research institutes at some point in their careers. Their colleagues who formed the HSE core came directly from RAS institutes and MSU. In Ekateriburg, Nesterova, Sabirianova, and Kadochnikov defended their dissertations at the Ural Branch of the RAS. Bogolyubova, as well as several of her Siberian colleagues, were cyberneticists. There was also an MSU graduate in cybernetics at Ural State. If the affiliations with the RAS and MSU bestowed luster on academic credentials, they were also a well-recognized stamp of quality. Similarly, a degree in cybernetics was a sign of elite economic education. Furthermore, an abstract science, math was considered more scientific and rational than Marxist political economy. In short, from its higher scientific ground, universalistic mathematics was viewed as superior to particularistic Soviet economic approaches.

Besides convincing colleagues of the appropriateness of their pursuit, the innovators' credentials brought support from the international academic community and influential political figures in Russia. The European Commission grants and the goodwill of the Russian Ministers proved crucial for the entire HSE enterprise during its formative years. The reputation of the MSU EF professors made the Faculty an attractive partner for international collaboration. It is not accidental that the first retraining institute of Russian economists was organized by the World Bank together with Moscow State. In Ekaterinburg, grants from the European Commission and Soros Foundation funded Nesterova's vision of USU EF development.

Translation and expansion of structures. As it was noted earlier, economics in Russia has two sources of legitimacy: Russian academia with its Soviet roots and the Western academic community. To mobilize the support of the Western academic community, the universities modified their structures so that they reflected the structures of Western universities. In this sense, Russian universities engaged in mimetic isomorphism of their international peers. However, the outcome of this mimicry was never a carbon copy of the original. Rather, it was a translation of the prototype, modified to fit the Russian context.

The cases trace the incremental addition of departments that gave new economic fields a formal organizational space. The restructuring and upgrading of the old departments was a less straightforward process. It involved assessing the departments' research agendas and programs for their relation to economics, modifying them, and possibly synthesizing their components with the new discipline. At a superficial level the upgrading also involved renaming.

Renaming. The renaming of existing departments is more complicated than it might seem because it occurred in at least two languages: Russian and English. In the Russian language, a name change often attests to the departments' parting with socialism. With its long tradition of research on socialist economies, the MSU EF provides ample examples of such changes when with the disappearance of socialism the names of departments and research labs lost their referents in the real world. In English, renaming involved interpreting the departmental activity in terms of Western economic science. In the process of interpretation, the department name would lose its Soviet character and became westernized. The USU EF translation of *ekonomika* and *khozyaistvo* is an example of this process. Since the two words are fundamental to economics in Russia, a brief excursus on their usage is appropriate.

There are two words in the Russian language to denote economy as a system and structure of economic life in the country. The first one, *khozyaistvo*, has Slavic roots and was widely used in Soviet discourse. With its Greek etymology, the second term, *ekonomika*, is recognizable in most European languages. Although in use in the Soviet Union, *ekonomika* gained prominence in the political discourse by the mid-1990s, gradually replacing *khozyaistvo*. If at the beginning of the political and economic reforms in 1987–1989, Gorbachev talked about improving the people's *khozyaistvo*, five years later his successor Yeltsin was engaged in improving the national *ekonomika*.

The shift in the use of the terms had a symbolic meaning: by virtue of its common European etymology, *ekonomika* is closer to the scientific discourse than *khozyaistvo* and therefore more rational. This shift, however, was slow to affect economic departments. When Ural State University introduced economics in the curriculum, it had two departments engaged in the study of world *ekonomika* and world *khozyaistvo*. As the USU EF began to make international contacts, the names of the two departments presented a problem: in English they were translated the same way. In order to avoid the confusion, the USU EF interpreted the departments' primary foci as world economy and international economics—the terms recognizable in the West.

Changing department organization and names involves structural and linguistic translation, which brings Western and Soviet systems side by side for the matching and modification of functions and meanings. Another type of change in the universities adapting economics consisted of expanding organizational boundaries to reach the world academic community.

Connecting to the world. Whether it takes the form of branches and joint degree programs or is metaphoric, geographic expansion effectively connects universities to their sources of legitimacy abroad. The Western academic community is both the authority on economics and a potential donor of financial and information resources. The HSE strategy of establishing joint degree programs illustrates both these roles. By uniting their degrees with the degrees of European universities, the HSE programs signaled that they are of the same quality. The prestige associated with Western degrees in Russia contributes to the image of the School. At the same time, joint degree programs often require travel of HSE students abroad, which the School would not be able to afford without agreements and partnerships with European universities.

The case of USU is another illustration of this point. Due to its geographic location and resources, Ural State has limited opportunities for student exchanges. To complement the existing exchange programs with Belgium and the Czech Republic, the USU EF partnered with the New School of Economics, an English-speaking diaspora of Western academia in Russia. Through the NSE's Russian and European professors, the USU EF entered international networks of economists.

The significance of interactions with the West is reflected in the universities' bureaucratic innovations. At the USU EF, Nesterova introduced the position of Assistant Dean for International Affairs, which was given to Sabirianova in 1995 after she visited the U.S. as a visiting scholar. The MSU EF Dean Kolesov hired an Assistant Dean for Public Relations. As HSE grew in size from one faculty to eleven, so did its administrative staff supporting international projects. By 2004 HSE had three non-academic departments whose sole purpose is to maintain, develop, and plan collaborative projects with Western Europe and North America.

Thus, in the process of adapting economics, the universities modified their organization by adding and restructuring academic departments, expanding their boundaries abroad, and establishing auxiliary positions and offices to maintain and stretch these boundaries further. These changes concern the universities spatial contexts. In addition, as the stories and enthymemes suggest, the universities altered their temporal contexts, i.e., their histories. Revising organizational histories, reshuffling the facts, forgetting episodes involves changing the meanings attached to these histories, facts, and episodes. Hence, they are symbolic.

Organizational histories and identities. In the universities' stories and enthymemes, the organizational time continuum is pliable. MSU and USU alter time to emphasize positive features of the Soviet past or suspend Soviet decades from their history. HSE stretches its history to connect to the histories of Western universities and grafts itself onto them. Making organizational environments more receptive of economics, these manipulations also preserve the most cherished features of organizational identity. For MSU, the cherished feature is the monumental Soviet tradition, for USU it is only part of it: the Soviet mathematical school. At the HSE, it is the pro-Western orientation of its founders.

As shared values and meanings, the universities' identities function as Perrow's (1986) premise controls: they carry tacit and taken for granted knowledge that organizational members use to interpret problems, innovations, events, and processes. In other words, people use them in making sense of situations (Weick, 1995). The enthymemes show how the MSU faculty and administrators perceive Western teaching methods through the prism of the Soviet tradition and judge them inferior when they differ from Soviet methods. USU faculty members, administrators, and graduates look at economics through the lens of the Soviet mathematical school and see the common math foundations of the Western and Soviet sciences. Having accepted Western universities as models for emulation, HSE is suspicious of everything that is Soviet.

These lenses and prisms, forming and directing the organizational vision, create a mental world map that guides the academics' interpretation of reality. This mental world map is what Ranson, Hinings and Greenwood (1980), following Giddens (1979) and Schulz (1967), call interpretative schemes. The concept of interpretative schemes is helpful in understanding the symbolic changes that occurred in the universities in the early 1990s and led to the adoption and adaptation of Western economics. It is also useful in explaining why the universities could no longer keep their histories intact and had to alter them to de-emphasize the Soviet past.

The MSU case analysis revealed that the Soviet tradition as a set of institutionalized routines and rules contained the possibility of change. Gradually, over the last decade, MSU absorbed new elements: it expanded the organizational and curricular structure, retrained its faculty in new economic specializations, and introduced Western methods of teaching. However, initially in the early 1990s the rapidly disintegrating socialist economy and the advent of the market came as a shock to the majority of Soviet academic economists. The political and economic events that precipitated the introduction of market-based economics were too fast for the Soviet academics to prepare for the ideological shift in economic sciences. Therefore, the shift was radical.

Ranson and his colleagues (1980) observe that radical (as opposed to routine) transformations in organizational structures occur along with changes in the interpretative schemes of organizational members and that these changes are often stressful. In the Russian case, it was the transformations not in organizational but in disciplinary structures and content that caused initial stress and changes in the academics' interpretative schemes. Furthermore, as Bartunek found in her study of restructuring in a religious order (1984), the old interpretative schemes did not disappear entirely but were blended with and incorporated into new schemes. This resilience of the interpretative schemes and their ability to hybridize explains how at MSU and USU the acceptance of the Western discipline did not contradict the Soviet tradition. At HSE, the Western orientation of the university did not preclude it from drawing on the Soviet schools of mathematical and institutional analyses.

In addition to symbolic changes in their organizational histories and identities, the universities in the study created a compelling overarching story of economics as innovation. Along with modifications in the spatial and temporal contexts and rationalizations, the construction of overarching narrative is a rule of intercultural organizational translation (Sahlin-Andersson & Sevón, 2003). The narratives served to explain how and why the innovation was adopted, demonstrated why it was better than the status quo, and often contained compelling anecdotes about innovators. At HSE, such narrative was the foundation story, at USU it was two transition stories about students and mathematicians. At MSU it was the story of the Soviet tradition of excellence supported by the World Bank economic seminars in 1989.

The universities' active interactions with other organizations in the environment have been mentioned in the discussions of the innovators' sources of authority and the universities' geographic expansion. As the cases suggest, the Ministry and the UMO, as well as international philanthropic foundations played vital roles in the translation of economics in Russian universities. It is time, then, to have a closer look at the university environments and examine their key academic and non-academic actors.

Academic Actors in University Environments

The Ministry and the UMO. The cases and the overview of Russian higher education presented earlier in the book describe several key actors and sources of control in the field of economic education in Russia. One of the strongest formal ties of the universities in the academic environment is to the Ministry of Education. The Ministry approves the National Standards of Education that are legally binding for all state (public) educational institutions. The Ministry regulates higher education institutions through licensure and accreditation, which are made increasingly more complex to guard against newcomers to the field (Belov, 2002). And finally, the Ministry approves national reforms in education, which often leads to a redistribution of power among universities. For instance, the 2003 tug-of-war between MSU and HSE rectors over the course of reforms was accompanied by a courtship of the new Minister. Newspapers reported staged meetings and clandestine encounters between the rectors and the Minister who had yet to make a decision about his position (Kachurovskaya & Taratuta, 2004). The effort that the two powerful men put into winning the Minister's approval attests to the power of his office and shows how it exerts a coercive isomorphic pressure on the field of Russian education.

While the Ministry has the power to enforce law, the UMOs have the authority to impose norms of academic disciplines. The UMOs in economics are housed at MSU and HSE. As a classical university, according to the Russian classification of universities, MSU is the head of the UMO for Classical Universities in economics. Also a classical university, Ural State belongs to the same UMO. The HSE is the head institution for a more recently established UMO in economics and management. The two UMOs disseminate best practices in economic education and approve economics textbooks for publication. As gateways to the discipline, they determine the content for teaching and establish requirements for academic programs. These requirements are approved and disseminated by the Ministry as National Standards. Thus, as guardians and enforcers of professional norms, the UMOs are sources of normative isomorphism in the field of economic education. As head institutions of their respective UMOs, MSU and HSE are also sources of isomorphic pressures. In addition, through their faculty retraining institutes HSE and MSU disseminate their institutional models and practices to other Russian universities. On a smaller scale, the USU EF is engaged in similar activities through its summer schools for regional faculty.

Although the Ministry and the UMOs are powerful organizations, they do not control universities' actual activities. As Meyer (1992a) observes, in centralized systems of education, the decoupling of formal authority from activities is often greater than in decentralized systems like U.S. higher education. A good illustration of such decoupling is the origins of the baccalaureate at the MSU Economic Faculty.

The official history of the MSU EF published in the Faculty periodicals proudly reports that the MSU EF was the first in the country to replace the Soviet five-year specialist with Bachelor's and Master's programs. The Faculty admitted the first students to Bachelor's and Master's programs in

1991. What is remarkable about the date is that the Ministry would provisionally allow universities to experiment with a baccalaureate only a year later, in 1992. The law officially granting Bachelor's and Master's programs a legal status appeared in 1994. It follows, therefore, that for a year the MSU EF taught students in a legal vacuum.

The story illustrates at least two points. First, the Ministry did not fulfill its primary responsibility of enforcing law and banning the MSU innovation. The authority of the Ministry was effectively decoupled from the activities of its subordinate institution. Second, in that particular situation, MSU had more authority than its superior in the administrative hierarchy. Moreover, it is likely that the Ministry's provisional permission to all Russian universities to experiment with new programs was due to the influence of Moscow State University.

The decoupling of the formal authority and organizational activity also increased the flexibility of the universities' responses to changes in the environment. The MSU EF Dean Kolesov experimented with organizational forms on his own without being penalized by the Ministry. The USU EF Dean Nesterova disregarded the UMO's recommendations as outdated and followed her own mind in program design.

Western academia as a source of isomorphism. The Russian academic environment is not the only source of isomorphic pressures. Since Western academic communities are regarded as sources of authority on economics, Russian universities adapting the discipline also had to accommodate professional norms, practices, and structures that have guided its development in the West. Although adaptation of Western practices is couched in the discourse of rationalization, it is not clear to what extent these innovations have constituted improvements. For example, after a year at a U.S. university, Sabirianova returned to Ural State and persuaded her colleagues to replace oral examinations with written tests. It also happened that during the same year, the Ministry changed Standards for programs in economics and required that students be re-taught according to the new standard. Sabirianova's colleagues found themselves in a situation where they had twice as many students as they usually had. Nevertheless, they pioneered written forms of evaluation as better assessment tools for their subjects, despite their initial inefficiency in grading, which was seldom officially recognized.

The adoption of an innovation for the sake of appropriateness rather than efficiency has been noted by many institutionalist scholars (e.g., DiMaggio and Powell, 1991b; Meyer and Rowan, 1991; Meyer and Zucker, 1989). It was also observed that a hasty short-term adoption may result in a 'lock-in' where organizations cannot develop it further over time (Stark, 2001). In the Russian case it is difficult to determine to what extent these propositions apply to the universities' adoption of written tests. In the U.S. academic community, written tests in economics are critiqued for their inefficiency and narrow focus (Walstad, 2001). In the Russian universities' stories and enthymemes, written tests are praised for their objectivity and efficiency but criticized for replacing the Soviet tradition of oral examinations. It appears therefore that their legitimacy as evaluation tools is not in doubt in Russian universities. Rather, it is their cultural appropriateness that is in question.

Stretched over large geographic areas, the Russian higher education and Western academic communities constitute only part of the institutional environment of the universities in the study. Meyer (1992d) suggests that the field of education goes beyond the boundaries of individual schools and includes non-educational organizations and groups. In a similar vein, Knorr-Cetina (1981, p. 82) proposes that the context of science consists of "trans-scientific fields" or networks of symbolic relationships that exceed the boundaries of scientific communities.

Allies in the Political, Social, and Economic Spheres at Home and Abroad

Analyzing the role of non-academic supporters of science, Latour (1999) calls them allies. This term stresses the political nature of interactions between scientific fields and their supporters in the political, economic, and social spheres. The founding story of the Higher School of Economics illustrates this point.

When in 1989 Kuzminov and Yasin wanted to introduce courses in economics at their native MSU EF, the Faculty administration was unsupportive. Their attempts failed similarly in other MSU departments and at the Physical Technical Institute. By 1992, when they began to advocate the idea of a new school, they had no allies within universities. Moreover, they had a strong opposition: the MSU EF opened their Bachelor's and Master's programs a year before and did not want any competition. Support came first from Gaidar who was a prominent member of President Yeltsin's Cabinet, then from the European Union. An academic economist and architect of an unpopular transition to market reform, Gaidar was a controversial figure in Russian politics of the time. He was perceived as a westernizer. For Kuzminov and Yasin, receiving support from this particular official meant further distancing themselves from the Soviet academic establishment. The grant from the European Commission's Tacis Program and the French government was both validation of their vision of the school and of their credentials. Thus, in the HSE case, the non-academic allies played a greater role than academia in the School's foundation and formative years.

As the cases show, HSE was not the only school in the study that benefited from the support of the European Commission Tacis Program. At various years in their development, all three universities received Tacis grants. Like its sister program Tempus, Tacis targets the members of Newly Independent States for collaborative projects with Europe. Competing for the same grants, the universities develop overlapping networks of supporters in Europe. For instance, a French professor Mihail Sollogub who is quoted saying that HSE is a French-Russian child was also active in assisting the MSU EF with its curricular reforms. Much respected by his MSU colleagues, Sollogub is also a member of the HSE Academic Council.

The HSE double link to the Ministry of Education and the Ministry of Economic Development is an example of a formal incorporation of a non-academic structure by the university. The patronage of the Ministry of Economic Development added stability to HSE's financial well-being and safeguarded it from excessive control by the first Ministry.

All three universities in the study have established ties with the government, local corporations, firms, and industrial enterprises whose CEOs and directors are invited as guest lecturers. In Moscow, the invited speaker list includes ministers and heads of multinational corporations. In Ekaterinburg, it consists of the members of the governor's cabinet, regional industrialists and businessmen. Besides enhancing the practical aspects of economic education, these ties lead to research grants for faculty and internship opportunities for students. For example, HSE has formal internship agreements with the Arthur Andersen Firm and Russian corporation LogoVaz. In addition to internships, the two enterprises established scholarships for HSE students.

Thus, university alliances with European grant-giving organizations and leading Russian figures in the government, industry, and business provide schools with authority and resources to support their adaptation of economics. However, the Latourian five-loop model of a scientific field would not be complete without consideration of another player in the external environment: the public.

Public Relations

The inclusion of the public in the conceptualization of a scientific field may seem like a stretch. However, what Latour (1999) claims is not an invasion of classrooms and labs by nonacademic people. Rather, he intends to emphasize the role that the public opinion plays in the life of scientific fields. As a scientific and academic field, economics is not immune to the opinions of people about economic research and education. The angry newspaper articles of the early 1990s blamed economists for bad science that failed to cure the deteriorating economy. The public outcry about Gaidar's neoliberal reforms cost him his position as the Minister of Economy and Finance and tarnished liberal economic models as socially destructive. In the field of education, although the demand for economists has been on the rise since the early 1990s, so has the number of vocational schools, institutes, and universities that opened programs in economics.

In these circumstances, MSU, HSE, and USU had to demonstrate that their education indeed gave useful economic knowledge and skills, which could be applied to real life and guarantee employment. The universities also had to signal to the community their contributions to the public good through research and policy making. For these purposes, all three universities established either a Public Relations (PR) position or a PR office. MSU and HSE also maintain websites where they post press releases and track articles about their respective institutions. As it was described in the cases, the confrontation between the MSU and HSE rectors generates a polemic on the philosophy of contemporary Russian education and is consistently covered in the press.

Thus, for the development of economics in Russia, it is important that the public appreciate the value of the Western discipline for the national economy and their own well-being. Furthermore, it is essential that the public have a favorable opinion about the universities as they adapt economics. As parents and citizens, people are supportive of those institutions that in their opinion have good academic programs and a reputation for advancing national science and education.

DISCUSSION OF INTERCULTURAL TRAVELS OF ACADEMIC FIELDS

The analyses of the translation of economics by three Russian universities offer glimpses of the multifaceted process of institutionalizing this academic field in Russia. The inquiry would not have been complete, had the research focused exclusively on the universities. Like the proverbial blindmen defining an elephant only by the body parts they can touch, the study would have left out key components of the complete picture. The cases, stories and enthymemes suggest that the process is both material and symbolic. Besides the traveling discipline and hosting universities, it involves academic and non-academic organizations, as well as people and the non-human world of economic models and theories. All components of the economic field are interconnected and one cannot exist without the other. For instance, economics could not have developed in Russia without a consensus among scholars about its legitimacy as a science. The Higher School of Economics would not have been founded without support from the government and the European Union. The market as it is understood today would not have been part of the public discourse without economics interpreting it in scientific terms. Parents would not have saved money to send their off-spring to MSU, HSE, or USU for proper economic education.

Thus, in order for it to develop as a field of scholarship and instruction, economics has to have a market and instruments to study it, a degree of consensus about its content in the academy, financial support and goodwill of powerful figures in the country, and understanding on the part of the public. In order for it to take roots in Russia, economics had to be decoupled from its Western contexts and translated into the organizational structure and language of Russian universities. The process of translation involved interpretation and modification, therefore economics in Russia is not entirely the same as economics in Europe and the U.S.

How does this picture of the adaptation of economics by Russian universities relate to the main question of this inquiry? In other words, how does it add to the understanding of intercultural travels of academic fields? It does so at least in three ways: by explicating the roles of translators and the process of translation, demonstrating that an academic field operates as a macro-actor, and delineating the role of narratives in translation.

Multiple Translators

Translation as a game of soccer. The translation of ideas is often compared to a ball game. For instance, Latour (1986) uses the metaphor of rugby. In a similar vein, Feldman and Pentland (2005) draw on the imagery of soccer. These scholars observe that before a goal is scored, the ball is kicked by multiple players. Receiving and passing the ball, players send it in different directions, adding their own interpretation (they decide *what to do* with the ball) and energy (they *kick* it) to the game (Latour, 1986; Feldman & Pentland, 2005). Ideas, practices, structures, and artifacts, or in general terms, a token also travels from one actor to another, moving in different directions propelled by the power that the actors invest in it (Latour, 1986). Handling the token and deciding what to do with it, the actors interpret it through the prism of their own interests and positions, modifying it in the process.

The metaphor of a ball game implies that the energy/power of all players in the game is equally important. Indeed, a soccer game is impossible if players stop kicking the ball. A chain of translation will be broken if actors lose interest in the token and cease interpreting it. In this sense, translation of economics in Russian higher education is not an accomplishment of one or two powerful actors but a collective achievement. The fact that Moscow State University is considered to be more powerful than Ural State University is irrelevant for the project of translation. What maintains translation is that the two universities are continuously engaged in interpreting and adapting the discipline to their own needs, interests, structures, and cultures, "bouncing it off" other actors (the Ministry, UMOs, universities, granting agencies, students, student parents, etc.) and receiving it modified by the new input and interpretation. Thus, the adaptation of economics in Russia may be viewed as a well-played match where the end result is an effect of hundreds of kicks, bends, and passes by multiple players.

Nonhuman translators. While a game of soccer is enacted by people, translation projects enlist human and nonhuman actors. Since organizations consist of people, personifying them is common in the organizational parlance: organizations are attributed personal qualities such as spirit (e.g., esprit de corps) and age (e.g., young, mature, ageing, etc.) and like people, they are endowed with agency (e.g. organizations make decisions, react to the environment, etc.). For instance, in their narratives, faculty members, administrators, and graduates characterized the universities in this study as young, old, innovative, or conservative, and described them as fighting corruption, defending traditions, and revitalizing higher education.

Personifying nonhuman phenomena, such as academic disciplines or market economies, is less accepted in the language, yet it is crucial for understanding the capacity of nonhuman actors to construct other actors, that are then enlisted in translation. For example, by providing definitions, categories, measurements, and formulae, economics constructs the market as people understand and enact it. Russians nowadays engage in activities that were unheard of in the Soviet Union: they buy land, assuming they can sell it; they own private enterprises, expecting to receive profits; and they conduct transactions in foreign currency, taking it for granted that some national currencies are more stable than others. These assumptions, expectations, and taken-for-granted knowledge of market relations are shaped by Western economic science, which thereby turns people into (market) economic actors. Economic actors, in turn, are interested in economics as a science that can predict and improve their financial well-being, thereby creating demand for knowledge about markets. Thus, economics produces economic actors, who in turn contribute to its maintenance and development.

Language as a nonhuman translator. Perhaps, most easily overlooked among nonhuman translators is a receiving language. The importance of language in cross-cultural translation is self-evident: after all, translation *is* a rendering from one language into another. However, linguistic translation implies that there is equivalence between the two languages, e.g., Russian translations of English textbooks are expected to say exactly the same thing as the originals but in Russian. This symmetry between the original and the translation is often impossible due to differences in the syntax and the cultural usage of vocabulary in two languages. Therefore, in the absence of a complete analogue of the token in the local vocabulary, syntax, and culture, the receiving language interprets it to fit what is available, modifying and transforming the original meaning. The adaptation of Western teaching methods by Russian faculty illustrates this point.

The universities in this study received many international grants for retraining their professoriate abroad. MSU and HSE are especially proud of the fact that almost all of their full-time faculty visited or studied at a Western university. From these visits abroad, Russian faculty members bring knowledge about various economic specializations, materials for designing courses at home universities, and collaborative projects with colleagues in other countries. They also bring Western teaching methods and practices. By the professors' accounts, Western education systems encourage active learning and individual research assignments in contrast to the Soviet model of education where students are passive recipients of information transmitted by teachers.

The experience of Russian faculty members as active learners of economics in Western universities is belied by the Russian language in translation to local university culture. When during the interviews I asked my respondents where and how they learned economics, they invariably began their answer with *nas nauchili* ('we were taught'). For an English speaker it would not be the first choice of answer to the question formulated in the active voice, yet passive syntactical constructions were prevalent in the professors' accounts of their student experiences in the West. As an architectural order of a language, the syntax arranges words into sentences, assigning the words to positions of subjects, predicates, direct and indirect objects, etc. Thus, the syntax establishes a hierarchy of relationships between subjects and direct objects: the subject is a strong doer of the action, while the direct object is a weak target of its actions. Therefore, in their answers, the choice of a subject or object position reflects the speakers' understanding of who has the power in a given situation. By choosing passive constructions, Russian faculty members subordinated themselves to the power of an invisible third person, the doer of the action, invoking and reproducing the Soviet model of students as passive and powerless recipients of knowledge. The receiving language distorted the original practice of active learning by translating it in a passive syntactical construction and neutralizing its meaning: active and passive canceled each other out.

To summarize, the chain of translators consists of human and nonhuman actors who contribute their interpretations to the transformation of the token during the processes of translation. These human and nonhuman actors can be placed within the network of economics as an academic field (see Figure 2.1). In the examples above, the conceptual core of economics occupies the center of the network, while a receiving language with its rules about sentence construction can be grouped with the nonhuman world of formulae, instruments, and artifacts.

Economics as a Macro-Actor

Latour's model of a scientific field adapted for the purposes of this study in Chapter Two (see Figure 2.1.) represents a *network* consisting of five flows of people, ideas, organizations, and artifacts. As was demonstrated in the integrative analysis, these people, ideas, organizations, and artifacts function as *actors* constructing structures, practices, procedures, and other organizations and ideas. Together, these actors share a common purpose: to ensure the translation and development of economics in the Russian context. Moreover, the *actor network* of economics in Russia is connected to actor networks of economics in other countries, notably, in Western Europe and the U.S., forming common projects, resources, and expertise. In the actor-network theory (Callon & Latour, 1981; Latour, 1999), "actor networks that coalesce in such a way that the whole is seen as having projects" (Feldman & Pentland, 2005) are called a macro-actor. In the geopolitical sphere, the European Union and the Newly Independent States are macro-actors. Among organizations and organizational fields, transnational corporations and industries may function as macro-actors (Feldman & Pentland, 2005).

As a macro-actor, economics is bigger and stronger than individual academic and educational institutions. When it traveled to Russian universities, it did not simply bring concepts and methods about the market. It arrived with a whole entourage of international communities of economists, Western organizations supporting economic education (e.g., Tacis, Tempus, the World Bank), and Western universities ready to lend their expertise to their Russian colleagues (e.g., Sorbonne, the London School of Economics, and the University of Rotterdam). Nor did economics come uninvited: in dire need of market economists, the reformers in Yeltsin's Government of the early 1990s welcomed it with the open arms. Once economics crossed the border to Russia after the country opened to the capitalist world, there was no force to halt its advance: the Soviet ideology that had banned Western economics as illegitimate knowledge rapidly deteriorated and could no longer censor foreign importations. Having settled down as a legal alien in select universities, economics soon became a naturalized citizen in the Russian academic states. The Ministry of Education officially acknowledged its legitimacy by issuing National Standards in economic education. Russian scholars recognized its validity as science and adapted it to the local economy in transition, creating transitional economics. Higher education institutions all over the country opened programs in the new discipline.

Thus, as a macro-actor, economics has been able to accomplish what economics as a discipline and as an educational program could not. As a macro-actor, it has interests and projects such as development and expansion in the academic territories of other disciplines. Employing the human and financial resources of its multiple networks, economics solicits support from other macro-actors (e.g., the French Government supporting reforms in economic education in Russia) and subdues the resistance of local organizations and universities, seducing them into cooperation with the ideas, practices, and resources of Western scholarly communities.

The transnational character of economics as a macro-actor indicates that economics is at home in many countries and cultures. However, the stories of faculty members, administrators, and graduates in this study suggest that this transnational residence may be problematic and that cross-cultural translation may invoke divisive identity narratives.

Organizational Identity Issues

Translation of foreign academic fields by local universities draws on and invokes multiple and competing identity narratives of varying size and scale. Universities have to decide how foreign innovations reinforce or transform their organizational histories and cultures, in other worlds, their sense of organizational self. For example, Moscow State University faculty members were concerned that Western economics and Western teaching practices would erode MSU Soviet traditions and westernize the University. By contrast, the Higher School of Economics was anxious to distance itself from everything Soviet and gladly accepted the label of a westernized institution. These anxieties and concerns manifested themselves in a controversy surrounding student evaluation methods.

Along with adapting Western content of economics and program structure, all three universities in the study converted to Western–style written exams, eliminating the Soviet practice of oral examinations. The replacement of oral exams by written ones precipitated numerous debates among faculty members, exposing larger philosophical and ideological issues with regard to institutional identities. The multiple direct and implicit meanings that the faculty, administrators, and graduates attributed to student evaluation methods are presented in the form of a semiotic chain analysis diagram in Figure 8.1.

A key assumption of semiotics as an approach to studying cultural communication and signification is that "surface signs are related to an underlying structure" (Feldman, 1995, p. 22). Applied to the case of evaluation methods in Russian economic departments, a semiotic analysis of written and oral exams uncovers worldviews and interpretative schemas of faculty and administrators. The diagram in Figure 8.1 is based on a semiotic chain technique, which consists of listing dichotomous direct meanings (denotations) and implicit meanings (connotations) of a phenomenon (Feldman, 1995). In this particular instance, the source of the direct and implicit meanings of student evaluation methods was MSU, HSE, and USU stories.

The lower part of the diagram summarizes the *direct meanings* of written and oral exams and their expressions in the university life extracted from the stories. In the stories, written exams are used at least in five senses: as a new evaluation method; as a sign of the integration in the world scholarly community; as an expression of Western ideology; as a proper evaluation tool; and as a destroyer of past achievements. In the logic of dichotomous thinking, oral exams carried the opposite meanings. The top part of the diagram shows connotations, or additional and implicit meanings underlying the direct meanings of written and oral exams. For example, when faculty members and administrators talked about oral exams as subjective evaluation tools (Meaning 4 in Figure 7.1), they invoked taken-for-granted notions about corruption of Soviet faculty (Connotation 4).

The five connotative continua at the top of the diagram represent these taken-for-granted and implied meanings that are invoked in the discussions of written and oral exams in Russia. On each side of the diagram, they form distinctly different worldviews. An organization or a person cast in the image of the left column is a westernized innovator who has moral principles and who is open to the world, yet wasteful of old achievements. Its opposite is a pro-Soviet traditionalist who is self-contained and who preserves the achievements of the past, yet lacks integrity.

The logic of opposition is such that there is no middle ground between the two ends of the continuum and by choosing one, the actor has to reject the other. Therefore, by choosing to advocate written or oral examinations, Russian economic departments and academics face dilemmas of subscribing

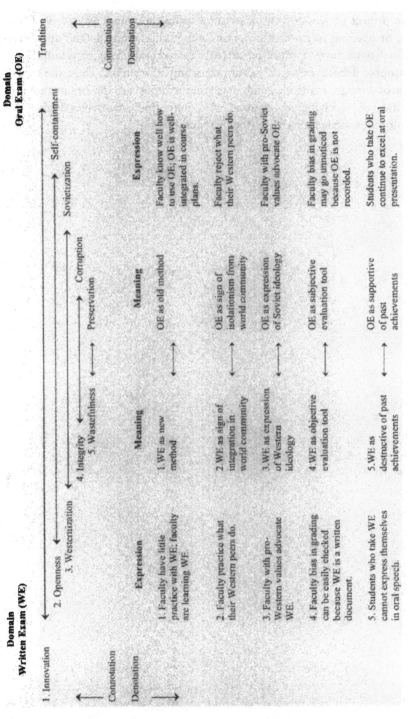

Figure 7.1. Semiotic Chain Analysis of Examination Methods in HSE, MSU, & USU Stories

to the project of westernization or supporting the native way of development, of opening to the world or remaining self-contained—the dilemmas
that in Russia have a tradition at least two-century long, crystallized in
philosophic debates between westernizers and slavophiles. Thus, the translation of foreign academic fields has ramifications for the organizational
identities of receiving institutions who may find themselves locked in
dichotomous interpretations of the new and the old.

Chapter Eight
Conclusion

The purpose of the study was to examine how economics as a Western field of scholarship and instruction is adapted by select Russian universities. Drawing on two constructivist strands of theories—social studies of science and institutionalism in organization studies—I examined the cases of three Russian universities that are ranked highly for their programs in economics. The cases were constructed from the official accounts of events recorded in university documents and supplemented with stories and enthymemes extracted from the interviews with faculty, administrators, and graduates of these universities.

While the purpose of the in-case analyses was to examine and explain the material and symbolic change processes taking place on individual campuses, the goal of the integrative analysis was to bring together the findings from all three cases in order to create a comprehensive picture of the adaptation of economics in the Russian context. Drawing on Latour's (1999) network model of scientific fields, I examined the changes in the disciplinary content structure, the Russian context, organization and culture of the universities adapting economics, their academic environment, their supporters in the political, social, and economic spheres, and public relations.

SUMMARY OF THE FINDINGS

The in-case analyses and the integrative analysis produced several key findings. The primary findings relate to the discipline of economics and universities adapting it. First, as I demonstrated in the cases, in Russia economics has been adapted through a combination of factors: an academic consensus about the legitimacy of the discipline; the existence of the market economy as an object of study; alliances in the political, economic and social spheres;

the support of Western philanthropic foundations, grant-giving agencies and universities; and a favorable public opinion about the discipline.

Second, from the cases, stories, and enthymemes I concluded that the universities adapting economics in Russia were engaged in the process of decoupling the discipline from its Western context and modifying its structure and tradition to fit their organizational contexts, while at the same time modifying their own structures and histories to suit the new discipline. As the result, as a scientific and academic field, economics in Russia differs from economics in the West: e.g., it uses different theoretical frameworks to study the local economy in transition.

In addition, I arrived at several secondary findings, which can be summarized as follows:

1. Economics, as a science studying market relations, participated in the construction of the market in Russia by creating a scientific discourse and theories explaining the country's turbulent transformations of the late 1980s and early 1990s as transitioning to the market. Once those unprecedented change processes were scientifically defined and classified in the terminology of economics, they ceased to be incomprehensible and uncontrollable. On the contrary, they became measurable and were directed toward the purposeful construction of the market.

2. The Russian faculty members who introduced economics in their universities drew on their professional authority to garner support for their colleagues and allies in the Russian government and Western communities. Common background characteristics of the innovators included an affiliation with MSU and the Russian Academy of Sciences or a degree in cybernetics.

3. Universities adapting economics drew on two sources of academic legitimacy: the Soviet tradition and the world academic community of economists.

4. The translation of economics into the structure of Russian universities was compounded by the difficulties of linguistic translation. Linguistic translation involves decision making with regard to selecting appropriate interpretations among options and emphasizing or de-emphasizing nuances of the meaning. As such, the linguistic translation of economics in Russian universities is political (e.g., the decision to continue the Soviet tradition of using the Slavic *khozyaistvo* or to replace it with the recognizably Western *ekonomika*).

5. In the process of translating economics in their organizational structure, the Russian universities modified their spatial contexts. They restructured and renamed old departments, added new academic and auxiliary departments, and expanded geographically.

6. The Russian universities adapting economics also changed their temporal contexts, i.e., they revised their past to soften or eliminate fragments of their history that might become barriers to the new discipline.

7. The Russian universities rationalize the adoption of economics and Western methods of teaching it. The rationalization can be positive, affirming that the innovation is improvement of the status quo, or negative, suggesting the opposite.

8. The universities in the study construct overarching narratives about economics, explaining the reasons and origins of its adoption and justifying it as a necessary and institutionally appropriate innovation. The overarching narratives in three Russian universities are represented by the stories regarding the founding of HSE, two USU transition stories involving students and mathematicians, and the MSU account of change founded on the Soviet tradition and supported by the World Bank.

9. Defined broadly as a set of tacit beliefs and assumptions guiding people's everyday understanding of the world, individuals' interpretative schemes changed along with the transformations of organizational structures. In the Russian case, the interpretative schemes of the faculty members changed as a result of structural and content transformations of economic science.

10. Old interpretative schemes do not disappear, rather, they incorporate new elements. This process explains how the faculty members at the classical Soviet universities, like MSU and USU, acquired elements of market thinking, while simultaneously retaining old Soviet interpretative schemes.

11. Interpreted as a set of routines, roles, and beliefs, the Soviet tradition contained the possibility of incremental change. This incremental change happens when during everyday re-enactment of the routines, new elements are absorbed, as evidenced by Moscow State University that gradually introduced Western practices while continuing to preserve Soviet academic traditions.

12. In Russia, support from actors in the Russian non-academic environment and Western academic community may be more important in founding a new university, than the support of the local

academic community. The founding story of the Higher School of Economics illustrates this point.

IMPLICATIONS OF THE STUDY

Theoretical Implications

The study has several theoretical implications. First, it demonstrates the viability of a theoretical framework that combines institutionalism in organization studies with social science studies. The double lens of such a framework broadens the scope of vision in investigations of academic disciplines adapted by universities and helps account for disciplinary and organizational change processes. Conceptualizing academic and scientific fields as interactive networks of ideas, people, organizations, and artifacts creates a comprehensive picture of academic and non-academic forces participating in the maintenance and development of disciplines. With translation conceptualized as the intercultural and interorganizational diffusion of innovations, the framework is attuned to the nuances of linguistic interpretation accompanying the intercultural movement of ideas and practices. The linguistic and cultural sensitivity of the framework suggests its applicability to other national contexts and education systems.

Second, the study suggests a research program on the adaptation of Western scientific practices by post-Soviet post-socialist academic institutions. So far, the studies of science and technology in the former Soviet Union have viewed the post-Soviet academic environment as inept at disseminating innovations (e.g., Martinsons & Valdemarsas, 1992) and as a source of 'brain drain'—a donor of scientists to the West (e.g., Rhea, 1992). In this study I take a different approach and provide a framework for analyzing Russian universities as active adaptors and disseminators of Western academic and scientific practices.

Third, the study adds to institutionalist theorizing about education by considering centralized education systems. For example, it confirms Meyer's (1992d) thinking about a significant decoupling of formal authority and organizational activity in centralized systems, as evidenced by Russian universities engaging in semi-legal activities despite strong ministerial control. At the same time, the study suggests modifications to existing theoretical propositions. For instance, Meyer (1992c) believes that in contrast to the U.S., the adoption of innovations in centralized education systems is less reliant on publicity, scientific justification, and moral reformism. The findings of this study do not support such propositions. The cases of the universities adapting economics demonstrate that they are actively engaged in promoting their economics programs and philosophies of education, propagating themselves as models of education in Russia, and advertising their status among Russian and international academic and non-academic communities. Furthermore, as the cases, organizational stories, and enthymemes show, these universities develop elaborate rationalizations for the adoption of the new discipline and couch their efforts in terms of conflicting Soviet and pro-Western ideologies. Therefore, drawing primarily on the analyses of secondary education, Meyer's (1992c) observations are not necessarily transferable to centralized higher education systems with their investment in scientific discourse and competition for students.

Fourth, as a study of intercultural organizational translation, the study establishes direct links with the discipline from which Scandinavian institutionalism initially borrowed the concept: linguistics. This study reflects on the nuances in the interpretation of economic specializations and department names, suggesting the political nature of the interpretation.

Practical Implications

The practical implications of this research project are oriented towards Western and Russian policy-making and grant-giving organizations and individuals who support education reforms in Russia.

First, the individuals and organizations supporting the development of new academic programs in Russia have to be aware of the uneven geographic distribution of higher education institutions in that country. The uneven geographic distribution has historically favored universities located in the European part of Russia and especially in Moscow and St. Petersburg, undoubtedly the best known Russian cities within Western academic communities. However, the overexposure of the two capitals to the West has obscured strong regional academic centers that have a long tradition of fundamental research and academic infrastructures. With different degrees of detail, this study described two such centers—Ural State University in Ekaterinburg and Novosibirsk State University in Novosibirsk—and demonstrated their roles in innovation adoption.

Second, scholars studying innovation adoption in post-Soviet and post-socialist countries suggest that professional communities and enterprises in these nations form closely knit informal networks that serve the same function as formal professional structures in the West (Stark, 2001; Xin & Pearce, 1996). The comparative analysis in this study draws a comprehensive picture of complex formal and informal Russian academic networks and key players in the field of higher education. In this sense, the book is a source of valuable background information for those individuals and organizations that may decide to form partnership agreements with universities in that country.

Third, Western supporters of education reforms in Russia need not be baffled by the universities' strong adherence to the Soviet tradition. As the case analyses show, the universities are selective in their interpretation of the past, emphasizing only those aspects of it that serve to strengthen their present position, e.g., strong preparation in mathematics, students' oratory skills, in-depth specialization, etc. As a foundation of past achievements and present development, the Soviet tradition is a symbolic anchor of certainty in the transforming economic, legal, and political environments of education. Furthermore, as evidence from the study suggests, universities with strong Soviet traditions nevertheless incorporate elements of the new thinking in their worldviews.

Finally, supporters of educational reforms in Russia need to be aware that in their eagerness to become part of Western academic communities, Russian universities may adopt Western models and practices uncritically. The current fascination with standardized tests and the disregard of their critique by Western scholars is one such example. At the same time, Russian universities may consciously be adopting Western innovations to meet their own particular needs, such as the elimination of bias and corruption in grading.

SUGGESTIONS FOR FURTHER RESEARCH

By design, I left several issues in this study unexplored. First, I purposefully abstained from examining the issue of the disciplinary content. My reluctance to investigate the conceptual core of economics in part reflects the tendency of social studies of science to avoid questioning the validity of scientific facts nevertheless assuming their social construction (e.g., Latour, 1999; Latour & Woolgar, 1979). A more important reason for this indifference to the subject is my disciplinary background. Although I sat in an undergraduate class in economics specifically for this project, I do not feel qualified to engage in the critique of Western economic theories and speculate about possibilities of their synthesis with Marxism. Therefore, an analysis of changes in the disciplinary content in the process of its translation to the Russian context is a fascinating research topic left to be explored by economists.

Second, my goals for this study did not include a comparison of the Russian higher education system with systems in Western nations. This topic, however, is pertinent to the institutional analysis of higher education. Ramirez & Meyer (1980) suggest that a research agenda for such analysis includes an examination of the origins, structure, and effects of education on the society.

Third, although my framework and design were informed by U.S. research on higher education, I deliberately abstained from applying the findings pertaining to American colleges and universities to the study of Russia's centralized post-Soviet post-socialist system of higher education. At the same time, there are several directions in which connections between the two can be explored.

One involves a comparative study of U.S. and Russian faculty teaching economics. Attempts have been made to apply the framework of Blackburn and Lawrence's (1995) comprehensive study of American professoriate to the analysis of Russian academic economists (Ivanov & Magun, 2004). At the same time there has been no systematic attempt to examine faculty differences and similarities in careers, professional values, norms, and expectations in two nations.

Another potential point of connection between U.S. and Russian research on education is the introduction of technology in teaching economics. In the U.S., the topic has been widely explored both in relation to teaching and to administration (e.g., Graves, Henshaw, Oberlin & Parker, 1997; Fink, 1997). In Russia, the interest in technology is mostly couched in terms of educational access and institutional development (Kuzminov, 2000; Tikhomirov, 2002). Since Russian universities adapting economics often work in continuous contact with their Western peers, a study examining the role of technology in the travel of disciplinary fields would be timely.

Yet another area of U.S. and Russian education research that can establish a fruitful dialogue is an analysis of higher education as a knowledge industry. In the U.S. the subject has been well explored (Peterson, 1997; Peterson & Dill, 1997), whereas in Russia it is relatively new (Reznick, 2001b). Given the dependence of economics in Russia on supporters from political, social, economic spheres and the government, the concept of knowledge industry may offer additional insights into the nature of the universities' interaction with their environment.

Fourth, focusing on state public universities, I alluded only briefly to the role of the private sector in the development of economics in Russia. However, students of private higher education assert that the flexibility of the private sector offers better opportunities for innovation (Lewis, Hendel & Demyuanchuk, 2003). Research on economics as a discipline in private universities could complement the findings of this study.

Finally, another direction of future research requires a closer communication between organization studies and linguistics. I suggest at least two directions for applying linguistics to the studies of innovation adoption and adaptation. First, an analytical tool needs to be designed for examining syntactical constructions of organizational narratives and their role in transforming ideas and practices during the translation process. Second, studies of the intercultural translation of innovations will benefit from a comparative analysis of the cultural usage of the vocabularies describing innovations in the native and receiving languages.

Appendix A

INTERVIEW PROTOCOL

1. What happened to the curriculum in your university in the last decade? (Probes: To the university curriculum? To the economic curriculum?)
2. What was the institutional climate like when the curricular change in economics started?
3. How did the curricular change in economics begin? (Probes: Who initiated it? Administrators? Faculty? Students? Ministry of Education? Precipitating event? How organized was the initial effort?)
4. What curricula models did your university use when designing a new academic plan in economics? (Probes: What if any other university curricula did you look at? Which curriculum served as a model? What was the role of the Ministry's Standards of Education directives?)
5. How was the curricular change in economics supported in terms of financial and human resources? (Probes: By the Ministry? Funding agencies? Internal resources?)
6. What were the barriers in the development and implementation of the new curriculum in economics?
7. Which components of economics curriculum were the easiest to implement? (Probes: Which courses? Content? Goals? Methods? Why?)
8. How relevant was the new economic curriculum to the Russian economy at the time of curricular change and how relevant is it now? (Probes: How did the university make it relevant to the Russian economy?)
9. How connected was the university to the world academic community at the time of the curricular change in economics and how

is it connected to it now? (Probes: Participation in professional exchange programs? International professional associations? Conferences? Availability of foreign journals and writings in economics?)

10. If you compare the economics curriculum at your university with the economics programs in Western universities, what would be similarities and differences?

11. How did the curricular change in economics affect the institutional climate and structure? (Probes: Did administrative styles change? What was the faculty's general attitude to the curricular change in economics? Were old departments reorganized? Have there appeared new units or departments?)

12. What does the university do to disseminate the economics curriculum in the region? (Probes: Is the new economics curriculum taught in the university's outreach programs? Do the economics faculty present it at national conferences? At workshops for junior faculty?)

13. How do the economics faculty and alumni participate in the development of economic policy at the regional or national level? (Probes: Do they consultant legislators? Municipal or regional government? National government? Do they work in business or industrial sector?)

14. Were you involved in the curricular change in economics and are you involved in it now? If yes, how? (Probes: (Were you on the faculty? What was your official position at the time of the curricular change?)

15. Is there anyone else I should talk with about the introduction of a new economics curriculum at this university?

Appendix B

DOCUMENTS EMPLOYED IN THE CONSTRUCTION OF CASES

10-letie V-Sh-E [The tenth anniversary of HSE]. (n.d.). Retrieved August 02, 2004, from the Higher School of Economics site http://www.hse.ru/10let/foto.shtml

Berezhkova, D. (2002, April 24). Obrazovanie, gosudarstvennye i negosudarstvennye obrazovatel'nye uchrezhdenia, dopolnitel'noe i biznes-obrazovanie v Rossii i Irkutskoi oblasti [Education, state and non-state educational institutions, continuing and business education in Russia and the Irkutsk oblast']. *Segodnya v Irkutske*, p. 1, 2, 5, 7.

Bobrova, A. (2002, April 24). Negosudarstvennoe obrazovanie v vide bel'ma na glazu [Non-state education as a cataract on the eye]. *Segodnya v Irkutske*, p. 4.

Bulgakova, N. (1998, January 9–10). Ras stupen'ka, dva stupen'ka [One step, another step]. *Poisk*, p. 10.

Echenike, V. H. (2001). Mezhdunarodnoye sotrudnichestvo fakulteta [International collaboration at the Faculty]. In V. P. Kolesov & V. P. Pankratova (Eds.), *Ekonomicheskii Fakultet 60 Let* (pp. 51–57). Moscow, Russia: Teis.

Ekonomicheskii fakultet [Economic Faculty]. (n.d.). Retrieved June 26, 2004, from Ural State University site: http://www.usu.ru/inform/?code=win&fac=14

Ekonomicheskii fakultet MGU [The MSU Economic Faculty]. (n.d.). Retrieved June 28, 2004, from Moscow State University site: http://www.msu.ru/info/struct/dep/econ.html

Ekonomicheskii fakultet MGU: znaniye i dostoinstvo [The MSU Economic Faculty: Knowledge and dignity]. (n.d.). Retrieved June 02, 2004, from the Moscow State UniversityEconomic Faculty site: http://www.econ.msu.ru/

Darya Vladimirovna Nesterova. (n.d.). Retrieved July 26, 2004, from the American Economic and Business Institute site: http://www.ramec.usu.ru/staff.php

Dezhina, I., Minin, B. & Libkind, A. (2001). Nuzhno li i kak ob'edinyatsya? [Shall on integrate and how?]. *Vysschee obrazovanie v Rossii, 6*, 12–20.

Dmitriy Valerievich Krutikov. (n.d.). Retrieved July 26, 2004, from the American Economic and Business Institute site: http://www.ramec.usu.ru/staff.php

Fakultet biznes informatiki [Faculty of Business and Computer Science]. (n.d.). Retrieved July 02, 2004, from the Higher School of Economics site: http://www.hse.ru/bisinform/

Appendix B

Fakultet ekonomiki [Faculty of Economics] (n.d.). Retrieved July 02, 2004, from the Higher School of Economics site: http://www.hse.ru/economics/default.html

Fakultet ekonomiki. Uchebnye plany [Faculty of Economics. Academic plans]. (n.d.). Retrieved July 02, 2004, from the Higher School of Economics site: http://www.hse.ru/economics/studyplans.html

Fakultet filosofiyi [Faculty of Philosophy]. (n.d.). Retrieved July 02, 2004, from the Higher School of Economics site: http://www.hse.ru/fakultet/filo/default.html

Fakultet gosudarstvennogo i munitsipal'nogo upravleniya [Faculty of Public and Municipal Administration]. (n.d.). Retrieved July 02, 2004, from the Higher School of Economics site: http://gmu.hse.ru/

Fakultet menegmenta [Faculty of Management]. (n.d.). Retrieved July 02, 2004, from the Higher School of Economics site: http://www.hse.ru/fakultet/management/

Fakultet mirovoi ekonomiki [Faculty of World Economy]. (n.d.). Retrieved July 02, 2004, from the Higher School of Economics site: http://www.hse.ru/fakultet/world_economics/

Fakultet prava [Faculty of Law]. (n.d.). Retrieved July 02, 2004, from the Higher School of Economics site: http://www.hse.ru/fakultet/law/

Fakultet prikladnoi politologiyi [Faculty of Applied Political Science]. (n.d.). Retrieved July 02, 2004, from the Higher School of Economics site: http://www.hse.ru/politology/

Fakultet psihologiyi [Faculty of Psychology]. (n.d.). Retrieved July 02, 2004, from the Higher School of Economics site: http://www.hse.ru/fakultet/psycology/

Fakultet sotsiologiyi [Faculty of Sociology]. (n.d.). Retrieved July 02, 2004, from the Higher School of Economics site: http://www.hse.ru/fakultet/sociology/

Fakultety i structura obrazovaniya [Faculties and the structure of education]. (n.d.). Retrieved July 02, 2004, from the Higher School of Economics site: http://www.hse.ru/fakultet/default.html

Federalnyi zakon ot 22.08.96 o vysschem i poslevuzovskom professional'nom orbrazovanii [Federal Law of 08/22/96 on higher and postgraduate professional education]. (1996, August 22). *Rossiyskaya gazeta,* p. 12.

Filippov, V. M. (1999). Ob itogakh raboty sistemy obrazovaniya Rossiyi v 1998 godu i osnovnykh zadachakh Ministerstva obshchego i professional'nogo obrazovaniya Rossiyskoi Federatsiyi v 1999 godu [On results of the work of Russian higher education system in 1998 and on main objectives of the Ministry of General and Professional Education of the Russian Federation in 1999]. *Vischeye i sredneye professionalnoye obrazovaniye, 4,* 1–23.

Gosudarstvennyi Komitet Rossiyskoi Federatsii po Vysshemu Obrazovaniyu. (1994). *Gosudarstvennye trebovaniya k minimumu soderzhaniya i urovnyu podgotovki spetsialista po spetsial'nosti 061400 "Kommertsiya"* [State requirements for the content minimum and level of preparation of a specialist in the specialization 061400 "Commerse"]. Moscow, Russia: The Russian Federation State Committee of Higher Education.

———. (1995). *Gosudarstvennye trebovaniya k minimumu soderzhaniya i urovnyu podgotovki spetsialista po spetsial'nosti 060100 "Ekonomechkaya teoriya"* [State requirements for the content minimum and level of preparation of a specialist in the specialization 060100 "Economic theory"]. Moscow, Russia: The Russian Federation State Committee of Higher Education.

———. (1995). *Gosudarstvennye trebovaniya k minimumu soderzhaniya i urovnyu podgotovki spetsialista po spetsial'nosti 060600 "Mirovaya ekonomika"* [State requirements for the content minimum and level of preparation of a specialist in the specialization 060600 "World economics"]. Moscow, Russia: The Russian Federation State Committee of Higher Education.

———. (1995). *Gosudarstvennye trebovaniya k minimumu soderzhaniya i urovnyu podgotovki spetsialista po spetsial'nosti 060700 "Natsional'naya ekonomika"* [State requirements for the content minimum and level of preparation of a specialist in the specialization 060700 "National economy"]. Moscow, Russia: The Russian Federation State Committee of Higher Education.

Higher School of Economics. (2004). *Lyubimov Lev L'vovich*. Retrieved July 02, 2004, from the Higher School of Economics site:

———. (2004). *Yasin Yevgenii Grigorievich*. Retrieved July 02, 2004, from the Higher School of Economics site: http://www.hse.ru/infopage/persona/ya/ yasin _ye_g.htm

———. (n.d.). *O V-SH-E*. [About HSE]. Retrieved July 02, 2004, from the Higher School of Economics site: http://www.hse.ru/rector_net/default.html

Hodjaev, A. Sh. (2001). *Podgotovka bakalavrov na ekonomicheskom fakultete MGU: desyatiletnii opyt transformatsii obrazovaniya* [Preparation of Bachelors at the MSU Economic Faculty: Ten years of experience in the transformation of education]. In V. P. Kolesov & V. P. Pankratova (Eds.), *Ekonomicheskii Fakultet 60 Let* (pp. 22–32). Moscow, Russia: Teis.

Inna Olegovna Maltseva. (n.d.). Retrieved July 26, 2004, from the American Economic and Business Institute site: http://www.ramec.usu.ru/staff.php

Informatsionnyi bulleten' Uralskogo Gosudarstvennogo Universiteta im. A. M. Gor'kogo [Information brochure of Ural State University named after A. M. Gorky (2004).]. Retrieved on July 15, 2004, from Ural State University site: http://www.usu.ru/#3

Istoricheskaya spravka [Historical note]. (1999.). Retrieved June 20, 2004, from the Higher School of Economics site: http://www.hse.ru/infopage/history.htm

Istoriya [History]. (n.d.). Retrieved June 02, 2004, from the Moscow State University Economic Faculty site: http://www.econ.msu.ru/cd.php3?id=8

Istoriya Moskovskogo Universiteta [History of Moscow University]. (2003). Retrieved June 28, 2004, from Moscow State University site: http://www.msu.ru/info/history.html

Itogovyi otchet o hode realizatsii pilotnogo etapa Megaproekta "Razvitiye obrazovaniya v Rossii" [Final report on the realization of the pilot stage of Megaproject "Development of Education in Russia"]. (1999). Retrieved July 26, 2004, from Ural State University Department of Economic History and International Economics site: http://www2.usu.ru/econom/kehis_econ/report/ Grant%20Report%201999.htm

Kalinina, T. N. (2001). Biznes—mirovozzrenie v uchebnom protsesse [Business is a worldview in the educational process]. In A. T. Tertyshniy (Ed.), *Vysshee obrazovanie v Rossii: Dostizhenia i perspektivy* (pp. 53–56). Ekaterinburg, Russia: Izdatel'stvo Uralskogo Gosugarstvennogo Ekonomicheskogo Universiteta.

Kirinyuk, A., Kirsanov, K. & Semchenko, E. (1999). Trudnosti rosta [Difficulties of growth]. *Vissheye obrazovaniye v Rossiyi*, *1*, 37–40.

Klara Sabirianova Peter. (n.d.). Retrieved July 26, 2004, from University of Michigan William Davidson Institute site: http://www.wdi.bus.umich.edu/faculty/klara_sabirianova.htm

Klikunov, N. & Okorokova, G. (2002). O statuse filiala [On the status of affiliation]. *Vysshee obrazovanie v Rossii*, *5*, 24–30.

Kolesov, V. P. (2001). Ekonomicheskomu fakultetu 60 let [The Economic Faculty is 60 years old]. In V. P. Kolesov & V. P. Pankratova (Eds.), *Ekonomicheskii Fakultet 60 Let* (pp. 5–21). Moscow, Russia: Teis.

Kolesov, V. P. & Hodjaev, A. S. (Eds.) (1997). *Katalog uchebnyh program ekonomicheskogo fakulteta MGU po napravleniyu "Ekonomika"1997–1998* [Catalogue of academic programs of the MSU Economic Faculty for Specialization "Economics," 1997–1998]. Moscow, Russia: Moscow State University, TEIS.

———. (1999). Spravochnik studenta 1999 [Student guide 1999] Moscow, Russia: Moscow State University, TEIS.

———. (2000). Spravochnik studenta 2000 [Student guide 2000] Moscow, Russia: Moscow State University, TEIS.

———. (2002). *Katalog uchebnyh program ekonomicheskogo fakulteta MGU po napravleniyu "Ekonomika"* [Catalogue of academic programs of the MSU Economic Faculty for Specialization "Economics"]. Moscow, Russia: Moscow State University, TEIS.

Kolesov, V. P. & Pankratova, V. P. (Eds.). *Ekonomicheskii Fakultet 60 let* [The Economic Faculty is 60 years old]. Moscow, Russia: Teis.

Kolichev, N. (1998, January 9–10). Diplom bez statusa [Diploma without a status]. *Poisk*, p. 14–20.

Kommentarii k federalnomu zakonu o "Visshem i poslevuzovskom professionalnom obrazovaniyi"[Commentary to the Federal Law on Higher and Postgraduate Professional Education]. 1998. Moscow: Informatsionno-Izdatelskii Dom "Filin" and Yuridicheskii Dom "Yustitsinform."

Kuzminov, Y. I. (2000, October 16). Tehnologia novogo ravenstva [Technology of new equality]. *Expert.*Retrieved July 02, 2004, from http://www.expert.ru/expert/special/educat/kuzminov.htm

———. (2003). *Challenges of education system modernization in Russia*. Retrieved July 02, 2004, from the Higher School of Economics site: http://www.hse.ru/rector_net/default.html

Loskutov, V. (2000). Slomannye nozhnitsy ekonomicheskogo obrazovania [Broken scissors of economic education]. *Vestnik Vysshei Shkoly*, *8*, 14–15.

Lyudmila Stanislavovna Ruzhanskaya. (n.d.). Retrieved July 26, 2004, from the American Economic and Business Institute site: http://www.ramec.usu.ru/staff.php

Megaproekt "Razvitiye obrazovaniya v Rossii. Programma podderzhki kafedr [Megaproject " Development of Education in Russia." Program of Departmental Support]. (2001). Retrieved July 26, 2004, from Ural State University

Department of Economic History and International Economics site: http://www2.usu.ru/econom/kehis_econ/report/Grant%20Mid%20Report%202001.htm

Mezhdunarodnoye sotrudnuchestvo GU-V-Sh-E [International collaborations of the State University Higher School of Economics]. (n.d.). Retrieved July 02, 2004, from the Higher School of Economics site: http://www.hse.ru/inter/english_version.shtml

Mezhdunarodnyi Institute Ekonomiki I Finansov [International Institute of Economics and Finance]. (n.d.). Retrieved July 02, 2004, from the Higher School of Economics site: http://www.hse.ru/ICEF/

Mezhdunarodnyi Simposium "Ekonomicheskaya teoria" [International Symposium "Economic Theory"]. (2004). Retrieved July 08, 2004, from Moscow State University Economic Faculty site: http://www.econ.msu.ru/ds.php3?id=339

Missiya Uralskogo Gosudarstvennogo Universiteta im. A. M. Gor'kogo [Mission of Ural State University named after A. M. Gorky (2004).]. Retrieved on July 15, 2004, from Ural State University site: http://www.usu.ru/#3

Nadezhda Pavlovna Bogolyubova. (n.d.). Retrieved July 26, 2004, from the American Economic and Business Institute site: http://www.ramec.usu.ru/staff.php

Natsional'naya doktrina obrazovania v Rossiiskoi Federatsii [National doctrine of education in the Russian Federation]. (1999, October). *Vuzovskie vesti*, p. 4.

Nauchnaya rabota [Research work]. (n.d.). Retrieved June 02, 2004, from the Moscow State University Economic Faculty site: http://www.econ.msu.ru/cd.php3?id=120

Obshchaya informatsiya: Rossiisko-amerikanskii institute ekonomiki i biznesa General information about the Russian American Economic and Business Institute]. (n.d.). Retrieved July 26, 2004, from the American Economic and Business Institute site: http://www.ramec.usu.ru/about.php

Obshchaya informatsiya: Uralskii Gosudarstvennyi Universitet [General information about Ural State University. Retrieved July 26, 2004, from Ural State University site: http://www.usu.ru/inform/?code=win&info=about

Ofitsialnye dokumenty 2003-2004 [Official documents 2003-2004]. (2004). Retrieved July 02, 2004, from the Higher School of Economics site: http://www.hse.ru/infopage/documents.shtml

Papenov, K. V. (2001). Nauchno-issledovatel'skaya rabota na ekonomicheskon fakultete [Research work at the Economic Faculty]. In V. P. Kolesov & V. P. Pankratova (Eds.), *Ekonomicheskii Fakultet 60 Let* (pp. 45–50). Moscow, Russia: Teis.

Programmy kursov [Programs of courses]. (n.d.). Retrieved July 26, 2004, from Ural State University Department of Economic History and International Economics site: http://www2.usu.ru/econom/kehis_econ/prog.htm

Rabochii plan po napravleniyu No. 521600 Ekonomika. Kvalifikatsiya Magistr [Academic plan for specialization No. 521600 Economics. Master's Degree]. (2001). Ural State University Economic Faculty.

Research Institute for Higher Education. (1998). Kontingent studentov gosudarstvennykh i negosudarstvennykh vuzov [Student enrollment at state and non-state higher education institutions]. *Magistr*, 5 (36). Retrieved January 25, 2003: www.informatika.ru/text/goscom/cinorgan/niivo/mag

Rossiiskii soyuz rektorov [Russian Rector's Union]. (n.d.). Retrieved July 28, 2004, from Moscow State University site: http://www.rsr.msu.ru/

Rossiisko-amerikanskii institute ekonomiki i biznesa [Russian American Economic and Business Institute]. (n.d.). Retrieved July 26, 2004, from Ural State University site: http://www.usu.ru/inform/?code=win&info=subdivisions/ramec

Russian Federation Law on Education. (1992). *Vedomosti Rossiiskoi Federatsii, 30,* 2221–2258.

Saveliev, A. & Romankova, L. (1998). O budushchei doctrine vyschego obrazovania [About the future doctrine of higher education]. *Vysshee obrazovanie v Rossii, 3,* 9–12.

Sergei Mihailovich Kadochnikov. (n.d.). Retrieved July 26, 2004, from the American Economic and Business Institute site: http://www.ramec.usu.ru/staff.php

Sillaste, G. (1999, February 7). Vse raboty khoroshi? [Are all jobs good?]. *Ekonomika i zhizn,'* 30.

Shatalin, S. (1990, September 8–14). Chelovek, svoboda, rynok [An individual, liberty, and market]. *Argumenti i Fakti,* pp. 1, 2.

Soderzhatelnyi otchet za 2000 po grantu No. HBC-803 2000 [Content report on grant No. HBC-803 for the year 2000]. (2000). Retrieved July 26, 2004, from Ural State University Department of Economic History and International Economics site: http://www2.usu.ru/econom/kehis_econ/report/Grant%20Report%202000.htm

Spravochno-informatsionnyi paket ekonomicheskogo fakuleta [Information package about the Economic Faculty]. (n.d.). Retrieved July 26, 2004, from Ural State University site: http://www.usu.ru/inform/?code=win&fac=14

Tatarinova, E. V. (2002). *Obrazovaniye v Sverdlovskoi Oblasti* [Education in the Sverdlovsk Region]. Ekaterinburg, Russia: Sverdlovskiy Oblkomstat.

Tatarkin, A. I. & Bochko, V. S. (2000). Integratsia akademicheskoi i vuzovskoi nauki kak osnova razvitia integratsionnyh protsessov v Uralskom federalnom okruge [Integration of academy and university sciences as a foundation for the development of integrative processes in the Urals Federal District]. In A. T. Tertyshniy (Ed.), *Vysshee obrazovanie v Rossii: Dostizhenia i perspektivy* (pp. 37–45). Ekaterinburg, Russia: Izdatel'stvo Uralskogo Gosugarstvennogo Ekonomicheskogo Universiteta.

Tatiana Vladimirovna Kulakova. (n.d.). Retrieved July 26, 2004, from the American Economic and Business Institute site: http://www.ramec.usu.ru/staff.php

Teleshova, I. G. (Ed.). (1996). *Magisterskaya programma "Ekonomicheskaya teoria"* [Master's program "Economic Theory"]. Moscow, Russia: Moscow State University, TEIS.

———. (1996). *Magisterskaya programma "Mezhdunarodnaya ekonomika i upravleniye"* [Master's program "International Economics and Management"]. Moscow, Russia: Moscow State University, TEIS.

———. (1996). *Magisterskaya programma "Matematicheskiye metody analiza ekonimiki"* [Master's program "Mathematical Methods of Economic Analysis"]. Moscow, Russia: Moscow State University, TEIS.

———. (2000). *Programma "Ekonomicheskaya teoria"* [Program "Economic Theory"]. Moscow, Russia: Moscow State University.

——. (2000). *Programma "Ekonomika firmy i otraslevyh rynkov"* [Program "Industrial Economics"]. Moscow, Russia: Moscow State University.

——. (2000). *Programma "Finansovaya ekonomika"* [Program "Financial Economics"]. Moscow, Russia: Moscow State University.

——. (2000). *Programma "Matematicheskiye metody analiza ekonimiki"* [Program "Mathematical Methods of Economic Analysis"]. Moscow, Russia: Moscow State University.

——. (2000). *Programma "Mezhdunarodnaya ekonomika"* [Program "International Economics"]. Moscow, Russia: Moscow State University.

——. (2001). *Programma "Ekonomicheskaya i sotsial'naya politika"* [Program "Economic and Social Policy"]. Moscow, Russia: Moscow State University.

Teleshova, I. G. (2001). Magistratura kak novaya forma podgotovki kadrov v oblasti ekonomiki i upravleniya [Master's program as a new form of cadre preparation in the field of economics and management]. In V. P. Kolesov & V. P. Pankratova (Eds.), *Ekonomicheskii Fakultet 60 Let* (pp. 33–44). Moscow, Russia: Teis.

Tikhomirov, V., Rubin, Y., Samoilov, V. and Shevchenko, k. (1999). Problemy prepodavaniya spetsial'nykh ekonomicheskikh distsiplin [Problems of teaching specialized economic disciplines]. *Alma Mater, 1,* 18–21.

Uchebno-metodicheskoye ob'edineniye po klassicheskomu universitetskomu obrazovaniyu Rossii [Academic methodological association for classical university education in Russia. (n.d.). Retrieved July 28, 2004, from Moscow State University site: http://www.umo.msu.ru

Universitet v tsyfrah i faktah [University in numbers and facts]. (2003). Retrieved July 02, 2004, from the Higher School of Economics site: http://www.hse.ru/statistika/default.htm

Uchebnyi plan po spetsializatsiyi No. 0601 Politiheskaya Ekonomika. Kvalifikatsiya Ekonomist, prepodavatel'politekonimii [Academic plan for specialization No. 0601 Political Economy. Qualification Economist and Instructor of Political Economy]. (1990). Ural State University Economic Faculty.

——. (1991). Ural State University Economic Faculty.

Uchebnyi plan po spetsializatsiyi No. 060100 Ekonomicheskaya Teoria. Kvalifikatsiya Ekonomist. Prepodavatel' [Academic plan for specialization No. 060100 Economic Theory. Qualification Economist and Instructor]. (1996). Ural State University Economic Faculty.

Uchebnyi plan po spetsializatsiyi No. 060100 Ekonomicheskaya Teoria. Kvalifikatsiya Ekonomist [Academic plan for specialization No. 060100 Economic Theory. Qualification Economist]. (2000). Ural State University Economic Faculty.

Uchebnyi plan po spetsializatsiyi No. 060600 Mirovaya Ekonomika. Kvalifikatsiya Spetsialist [Academic plan for specialization No. 060600 World Economics. Specialist Degree]. (1999). Ural State University Economic Faculty.

Uchebnyi plan po spetsializatsiyi No. 060600 Mirovaya Ekonomika. Kvalifikatsiya Ekonomist [Academic plan for specialization No. 060600 World Economics. Economist Qualification]. (2000). Ural State University Economic Faculty

Uchebnyi plan po spetsializatsiyi No. 521600 Ekonomika. Kvalifikatsiya Bakalavr [Academic plan for specialization No. 521600 Economics. Bachelor's Degree]. (1996). Ural State University Economic Faculty.

——. (2001). Ural State University Economic Faculty.

Uchebnyi plan po spetsializatsiyi No. 521600 Ekonomika. Kvalifikatsiya Magistr [Academic plan for specialization No. 521600 Economics. Master's Degree]. (1998). Ural State University Economic Faculty.

———. (2001). Ural State University Economic Faculty.

Uchebnyi plan po spetsializatsiyi No. 521612 Ekonomika. Programma buhgalterskii uchet, analiz, audit. Kvalifikatsiya Magistr ekonomiki [Academic plan for specialization No. 521612 Economics. Program in Accounting, Analysis, and Auditing. Master of Economics Degree]. (1998). Ural State University Economic Faculty.

Uchebnyi plan po spetsializatsiyi No. 521619 Ekonomika. Programma ekonomika firmy. Kvalifikatsiya Magistr ekonomiki [Academic plan for specialization No. 521619 Economics. Program in Economics of the Firm. Master of Economics Degree]. (1998). Ural State University Economic Faculty.

Uchebnyi plan po spetsializatsiyi No. 521621 Ekonomika. Programma matematicheskiye metody v ekonomike. Kvalifikatsiya Magistr ekonomiki [Academic plan for specialization No. 521621 Economics. Program in Mathematical Methods in Ecnomics. Master of Economics Degree]. (1998). Ural State University Economic Faculty.

Uralskii Gosudarstvennyi Universitet (1997). *Ekonomicheskii Fakultet, 1997–1998 uchebnyi god* [Economic faculty, 1997–1998 academic year]. Ekaterinburg, Russia: Ural State University.

———. (2001). *European Community Course Credit Transfer System: Informatsionnyi paket* [European Community Course Credit Transfer System: Information package]. Ekaterinburg, Russia: Ural State University.

Vladimirov, V. (2002). Organizatsionnaya struktura rossiiskih vuzov [Organizational structure of Russian institutions of higher education]. *Vysshee obrazovanie v Rossii, 5,* 5–11.

Yegor T. Gaidar. (2001). Retrieved August 02, 2004, from the Institute of Economy in Transition site: http://www.iet.ru/personal/CVgaidareng.htm

Zuev, V. M. (2001). Osnovnye napravleniya modernizatsii vysshei shkoly [Main directions of the modernization of higher education]. In A. T. Tertyshniy (Ed.), *Vysshee obrazovanie v Rossii: Dostizhenia i perspektivy* (pp. 3–8). Ekaterinburg, Russia: Izdatel'stvo Uralskogo Gosugarstvennogo Ekonomicheskogo Universiteta.

Appendix C

Stories From the Interviews Conducted at the Higher School of Econimics (HSE), Moscow State University (MSU), and Ural State University (USU)

Category	Story Topic	HSE	MSU	USU	Total
	Stories Included in Enthymeme Analysis				
1. Institutional roots & the beginning of transition to economics	Foundation	11	0	1	1
	Beginning of transition to Western economics	2	5	5	13
	Breaking point in the early 1990s: between the old and the new	0	0	9	8
2. Adoption & adaptation of the Western content and method	Use of foreign literature in course design	3	2	1	6
	Adaptation of the disciplinary content to the Russian context	1	6	12	19
	Practical relevance of economics to the Russian context	0	0	2	2
	Conflict b/w Soviet and Western approaches to economic education	1	2	1	4
	Adoption of Western teaching methods	1	2	2	5
	Curricular transformation in anticipation of economics	0	0	3	3

Stories From the Interviews Conducted at the Higher School of Econimics (HSE), Moscow State University (MSU), and Ural State University (USU) (contunued)

Category	Story Topic	HSE	MSU	USU	Total
	Stories Included in Enthymeme Analysis				
3. Training & retraining in economics	Traveling to the West for retraining and literature	6	6	6	18
	Going through retraining in Russia	5	2	5	12
	Organizing retraining for faculty from other institutions	2	3	1	6
4. Faculty	Brain drain of young faculty from academia	4	0	0	4
	Problems with old faculty	2	2	2	6
	Hiring young faculty	0	1	0	1
	Balance between old and new faculty	0	1	0	1
5. Students	Student involvement in curricular design	2	0	7	9
	Change in student population	0	1	1	2
6. Organizational development	Organizational growth and development	2	1	6	9
	Barriers to organizational growth	0	0	3	3
	Integration in the world scholarly community & international cooperation	2	2	4	8

Stories From the Interviews Conducted at the Higher School of Economics (HSE), Moscow State University (MSU), and Ural State University (USU) (contunued)

Category	Story Topic	HSE	MSU	USU	Total
	Stories Included in Enthymeme Analysis				
7. Economic education in the Soviet Union	Importance of the Soviet tradition in general	0	1	0	1
	Excellence in the Soviet teaching tradition	0	2	0	2
	High status of academic economists in the Soviet Union	2	0	1	3
	Democratism & collegiality of Soviet scientists	0	0	1	1
	Excellence in math preparation in the Soviet Union	2	2	2	6
	Excellence in fundamental (in-depth) preparation in the Soviet Union	0	1	1	2
	Conservatism of higher education in the Soviet Union	1	1	0	2
	Excellence of MSU faculty in the Soviet Union	1	0	0	1
	Excellence in MSU education in the Soviet Union (critical thinking skills & knowledge of foreign theories)	2	3	0	5
	Learning Marxism	4	2	0	6
8. Contemporary issues in the development of economics	Contemporary importance of math in economic education	0	0	3	3
	Economic research	1	0	1	2
	Relations b/w economists and Government today	0	1	1	2

Stories From the Interviews Conducted at the Higher School of Econimics (HSE), Moscow State University (MSU), and Ural State University (USU) (contunued)

Category	Story Topic	HSE	MSU	USU	Total
	Stories Included in Enthymeme Analysis				
9. Economic education in the Soviet Union	Preparing cadres for the future	1	0	0	1
	MSU's vindictiveness	2	1	0	3
	Unsupportive university administration	0	0	3	3
	Gender discrimination	0	0	1	1
	Loyalty to alma mater	0	1	1	2
	Total Included	60	51	94	205
	Stories Excluded from Enthymeme Analysis				
	Personal life and career	16	7	9	33
	(Im)possibility of theoretical synthesis between economics & Marxism	0	5	1	6
	General speculations	0	1	0	1
	Total excluded	16	13	10	40
	Total Stories	76	64	104	244

Appendix D

Coding Results for Reconstructed Enthymeme Premises and Conclusions, HSE

#	Theme	N
1	Designing new programs and courses	15
2	Establishing new programs and educational institutions	13
3	Faculty issues	12
4	Field of higher education in Russia	12
5	Economic education in the Soviet Union	12
6	HSE as a leading university	11
7	MSU as a leading Soviet university and HSE's rival	11
8	Adopting Western teaching methods and practices	10
9	Organizational growth and development	9
10	Learning economic disciplines	9
11	Adapting Western economic content	8
12	Teaching economic disciplines	8
13	Assessing and enhancing institutional quality	8
14	Good faculty	8
15	Marxist theoretical approach and ideology	6
16	Old universities	5
17	Russian economy	4
18	Leadership	4
19	Student issues	2
20	Integration in the world academic community	2
	Total	169

Appendix E

Coding Results for Reconstructed Enthymeme Premises and Conclusions, MSU

#	Category	How Many
1	Learning economic disciplines	18
2	Adapting Western models, methods, and practices	16
3	Designing new programs and courses	13
4	Economic education in the Soviet Union	12
5	Teaching economic disciplines	10
6	Faculty issues	9
7	Adapting Western economic content	8
8	Organizational development	8
9	MSU as a leading Soviet university	8
10	External influences on economic education	7
11	Integration in the world academic community	7
12	Assessing program quality	5
13	Importance of Soviet academic traditions	6
14	Faculty age	5
15	Organizational survival	5
16	Field of higher education in Russia	4
17	Marxist theoretical approach and ideology	4
18	Student issues	3
	Total	148

Appendix F

Coding Results for Reconstructed Enthymeme Premises and Conclusions, USU

#	Category	How Many
1	Faculty	45
	Quality of faculty preparation (n=9)	
	Faculty collaboration, teaching, and course design (n=14)	
	Faculty salary and motivation (n=5)	
	Problems with old faculty (n=11)	
	Faculty issues, miscellaneous (n=6)	
2	Establishing and maintaining programs in economics	29
	Program and curricular design (n=14)	
	Program structure (n=7)	
	Program quality (n=8)	
3	Students	
	Students' practical orientation (n=7)	
	Student involvement in curricular change (n=7)	
	Student research (n=4)	
	Student research (n=4)	
	Student issues, miscellaneous (n=8)	
4	The USU Economic Faculty	18
	Students and outreach at USU EF (n=4)	
	Quality, research, and curricular change at USU EF (n=8)	
	USU EF faculty (n=6)	
5	Adapting disciplinary content	18
	Content characteristics (n=12)	
	Content relevance to the Russian context (n=6)	

#	Category	How Many
6	Research	13
	Student research (n=5)	
	Faculty research (n=5)	
	Russian research grants (n=3)	
7	Peer universities and organizations supporting education	13
8	Course design	12
9	Teaching in economic disciplines	12
10	Economic education in the Soviet Union	9
11	Government and society	9
12	Marxist theoretical approach and ideology	7
13	Learning economic disciplines	8
14	Institutional norms	6
15	Mathematics in the Soviet Union	6
16	Universities in their environment	6
17	Program and institutional quality	5
18	Applied vs. theoretical knowledge	5
19	Organizational development and change	5
20	Barriers to organizational development and change	4
21	Adapting Western teaching methods and materials	4
22	Gender issues	4
23	Integration in the world academic community	3
	Total	271

Notes

NOTES TO CHAPTER ONE

1. This book is based on the dissertation study that I conducted in partial fulfillment of the requirements for the Doctor of Philosophy Degree at the University of Michigan, Ann Arbor.

NOTES TO CHAPTER TWO

1. Czarniawska (2004) made this observation with regard to the difference between Selznick's (1949) and DiMaggio and Powell's (1991b) approaches.
2. For a more comprehensive analysis of differences between the old and the new institutionalist traditions in organization studies, please, see DiMaggio & Powell (1991a).
3. In a similar vein, Clark (1983) proposed a tripartite model of higher education, consisting of three forces shaping and regulating higher education institutions: state authority, the market, and academic oligarchy. Based on new institutionalist conceptualizations of organizational fields, Clark's model anticipates later institutionalist works that explicate coercive pressures of the government and the normative pressures of professionalization as coercive and normative isomorphism (e.g., DiMaggio & Powell, 1991b).
4. Meyer and Rowan (1991) acknowledge another source of isomorphism: technical exchanges and interdependencies between organizations and environments. However, for the purpose of their analysis, they choose not to pursue it.

NOTES TO CHAPTER THREE

1. The details are withdrawn to protect the identities of the respondents.
2. There exist two schools of thought about overlapping data collection with data analysis. Unlike Eisenhardt (1989) who recommends it, Feldman (1995) believes that the two stages should not be blurred because the overlapping of the two may prematurely narrow the focus of the research. This

study heeds Feldman's warning in that it plans Phase 3 as a peer check and clarification stage after the data collection in Phase 2.

NOTES TO CHAPTER FOUR

1. Scientific atheism drew on Marxist political philosophy to debunk world religions.
2. In the Soviet Union, the official name of the Academy was the Academy of Sciences of the U.S.S.R. It was renamed the Russian Academy of Sciences after the collapse of the Soviet Union.
3. This discussion and Table 4.1 draw on the list of economic fields as described in the Journal of Economic Literature Classification System (n.d.).

NOTES TO CHAPTER FIVE

1. The concept of an academic or classical university in Russia is similar to the US definition of a research university, according to the Carnegie Classification.
2. This discussion and Table 5.1 draw on the list of economic fields as described in the Journal of Economic Literature Classification System (n.d.).

NOTES TO CHAPTER SIX

1. This discussion and Table 6.1 draw on the list of economic fields as described in the Journal of Economic Literature Classification System (n.d.).

NOTES TO CHAPTER SEVEN

1. Duma is the name of the Russian Parliament.

Bibliography

Alexeev, M., Gaddy, C. & Leitzel, J. (1992). Economics in the former Soviet Union. *Journal of Economic Perspectives, 6,* 137–148.

Altbach, P. G. (1978). The distribution of knowledge in the Third World: A case study in neocolonialism. In P. G. Altbach & G. P. Kelly (Eds.), *Education & colonialism* (pp. 301–331). New York: Longman.

———. (1982). *Higher education in the Third World: Themes and variations.* Singapore: Koon Wah Printing Pte. Ltd.

———. (1998). *Comparative higher education: knowledge, the university, and development.* Greenwich, CT: Ablex Publishing Corporation.

Appadurai, A. (2000). Disjuncture and difference in the global cultural economy. In D. Held & A. McGrew (Eds.), *The global transformations reader: An introduction to the globalization debate* (pp. 230–239). Cambridge, U.K.: Polity Press.

Argumenti i Fakti. (1991). Tolko dlya chitatelei "AIF" [Only for the readers of AIF], 43, p. 1.

Aristotle. (1953). Rhetoric. In T.A. Moxon (Ed.), *Aristotle's poetics and rhetoric.* New York: Everyman's Library.

———. (1995). Rhetoric. In J. Barnes (Ed.), *The complete works of Aristotle.* Princeton, NJ: Princeton University Press.

Ashmore, M., Myers, G., & Potter, J. (1995). Discourse, rhetoric, reflexivity: Seven days in library. In S. Jasanoff, G.E. Markle, J.C. Petersen & T. Pinch (Eds.), *Handbook of science and technology studies* (pp. 321–343). Thousand Oaks, CA: Sage.

Bain, O. B., Zakharov, I. A. & Nosova, N. B. (1998). From centrally mandated to locally demanded service: The Russian case. *Higher Education, 35,* 49–67.

Bartunek, J. (1984). Changing interpretative schemes and organizational restructuring: The example of a religious order. *Administrative Science Quarterly, 29,* 355–372.

Becher, T. (1987). The disciplinary shaping of the profession. In B. Clark (Ed.), *The academic profession* (pp. 271–304). Berkley, CA: University of California Press.

———. (1989). *Academic tribes and territories: Intellectual inquiry and the cultures of disciplines.* Bristol, PA: Open University Press.

Belov, V. (2002). Sistema otsenki kachestva obrazovaniya [System of educational quality evaluation]. *Vyssheye Obrazovanie v Rossii, 1,* 44–49.

Bensabat, I., Goldstein, D. K., & Mead, M. (1987). The case research strategy in studies of information systems. *MIS Quarterly, 11,* 369–386.

Berger, P. L. & Luckmann, T. (1966). *The social construction of reality: A treatise in the sociology of knowledge.* New York: Doubleday.

Blackburn, R. T. & Lawrence, J. H. (1995). *Faculty at work: Motivation, expectation, satisfaction.* Baltimore & London: John Hopkins University Press.

Boje, D. (1991). The storytelling organization: A study of story performance in an office supply firm. *Administrative Science Quarterly, 36* (1), 106–126.

Bourdieu, P. (1980). *The logic of practice.* Stanford, CA: Stanford University Press.

———. (1991). The peculiar history of scientific reason. *Sociological Forum, 6* (1), 3–26.

Brint, S. & Karabel, J. (1991). Institutional origins and transformations: The case of American community colleges. In W. W. Powell & P. DiMaggio (Eds.), *The new institutionalism in organizational analysis* (pp. 337–360). Chicago, IL.: The University of Chicago Press.

Brooker, R. & Macdonald, D. (1999). Did we hear you?: Issues of student voice in a curriculum innovation. *Journal of Curriculum Studies, 31* (1), 83–97.

Brue, S.L. & MacPhee, C. R. (1995). From Marx to markets: Reform of the university economics curriculum in Russia. *Journal of Economic Education, 26,* 182–194.

Callon, M. & Latour, B. (1981). Unscrewing the big Leviathan: How actors macrostructure reality and how sociologists help them to do so. In K. Knorr-Cetina & A. V. Cicourel (Eds.), *Advances in social theory and methodology* (pp. 277–303). London: Routledge and Kegan Paul.

Cameron K.S. (1984). Organizational adaptation and higher education. *Journal of Higher Education, 55,* 122–144.

Camiah, N. & Hollinshead, G. (2003). Assessing the potential for effective crosscultural working between "new" Russian managers and western expatriates. *Journal of World Business, 38,* 245–61.

Canning, M., Moock, P. & Heleniak, T. (1999). *Reforming education in the regions of Russia. World Bank Technical Paper No. 457.* Washington, D.C.: The World Bank.

Castells, M. (1999). Flows, networks, and identities: A critical theory of the information society. In M. Castells, R. Flecha, P. Freire, H. A. Giroux, D. Macedo & P. Willis (Eds.), *Critical education in the new information age* (pp. 37–65). Lanham, MD: Rowman & Littlefield Publishers.

———. (2000). The network society. In D. Held & A. McGrew (Eds.), *The global transformations reader: An introduction to the globalization debate* (pp.76–82). Cambridge, U.K.: Polity Press.

Clark, B. R. (1956). *Adult education in transition.* Berkley, CA: University of California Press.

———. (1972). The organizational saga in higher education. *Administrative Science Quarterly, Vol. 17* (2): 178–184.

———. (1983). *The higher education system: Academic organization in crossnational perspective.* Los Angeles, CA: University of California Press.

Clark, P. & Staunton, N. (1990). *Innovation in technology and organization.* London: Routledge.

Clarke, R. (1985). *Science and technology in world development.* Oxford, New York: Oxford University Press/UNESCO.

Coleman, J. C. & Court, D. (1993). *University development in the Third World: the Rockefeller Foundation experience.* Oxford & New York: Pergamon Press.

Crane, D. (1972). *Invisible colleges: Diffusion of knowledge in scientific communities.* Chicago, IL: University of Chicago Press.

Creswell, J. W. (1994). *Research design: Qualitative and quantitative approaches.* Thousand Oaks, CA: Sage.

Cutcliffe, S. H. (2000). *Ideas, machines, and values: An introduction to science, technology, and society studies.* Lanham, MD: Rowman & Little Publishers.

Czarniawska, B. (1997). *Narrating the organization: Dramas of institutional identity.* Chicago, IL: Chicago University Press.

———. (2004). *On time, space, and action nets.* Gothenburg Research Institute, Göteborg University. Unpublished manuscript.

Czarniawska, B. & Joerges, B. (1996). Travel of ideas. In B. Czarniawska & G. Sevón (Eds.), *Translating organizational change* (pp. 13–48). Berlin and New York: Walter de Gruyter.

Czarniawska, B. & Sevón, G. (1996). Introduction. In B. Czarniawska & G. Sevón (Eds.), *Translating organizational change,* (pp. 1–13). Berlin and New York: Walter de Gruyter.

Damanpour, F. (1987). The adoption of technological, administrative, and ancillary innovations: Impact of organizations factors. *Journal of Management, 13,* 675–688.

———. (1990). Innovation effectiveness, adoption and organizational performance. In M. West & J. L .Farr (Eds.), *Innovation and creativity at work: Psychological and organizational strategies* (pp. 125–141). New York: John Wiley & Sons.

David-Fox, M. (1997). The emergence of a 1920s academic order in Soviet Russia. *East/West Education, 18,* 106–142.

Denzin, N. K. & Lincoln, Y.S. (2000). Introduction: The discipline and practice of qualitative research. In N. K. Denzin & Y. S. Lincoln (Eds), *Handbook of qualitative research* (2nd edition) (pp. 1–28). Thousand Oaks, CA: Sage.

DiMaggio, P. (1988). Interest and agency in institutional theory. In L. G. Zucker (Ed.), *Institutional patterns and organizations,* (pp. 3–22). Cambridge, MA: Ballinger.

DiMaggio, P. & Powell, W. W. (1991a). Introduction. In W. W. Powell & P. DiMaggio (Eds.), *The new institutionalism in organizational analysis,* (pp. 1–38). Chicago, IL: The University of Chicago Press.

———. (1991b). The iron cage revisited: Institutional isomorphism and collective rationality in organizational fields. In W. W. Powell & P. DiMaggio (Eds.), *The new institutionalism in organizational analysis* (pp. 63–83). Chicago, IL: The University of Chicago Press.

Eisenhardt, K. M. (1989). Building theories from case study research. *Academy of Management Review, 14,* 532–550.

Epper, R. M. (1997). Coordination and competition in postsecondary distance education: Comparative case study of statewide policies. *Journal of Higher Education, 68,* 551–587.

Feldman, M. S. (2004). Making sense of stories: A rhetorical approach to narrative analysis. *Journal of Public Administration Research and Theory, 14,* 147–170.

———. (1989). *Order without design: Information production and policy making.* Stanford, CA: Stanford University Press.

———. (1995). *Strategies for interpreting qualitative data.* Thousand Oaks, CA: Sage.

Feldman, M. S., Bell, J., & Berger, M. T. (Eds.), (2003). *Gaining access: A practical and theoretical guide for qualitative researchers.* Walnut Creek, CA: Altamira Press.

Feldman, M. S. & Pentland, B. T. (2003). Reconceptualizing organizational routines as a source of flexibility and change. *Administrative Science Quarterly, 48,* 94–118.

———. (2005). Organizational routines and the macro-actor. In B. Czarniawska, & T. Hernes (Eds), *Organizing and the macro-actor.* Forthcoming.

Feldman, M. & Sköldberg, K. (2002). Stories and the rhetoric of contrariety: Subtexts of organizing (change). *Culture and Organization, 8* (4), 275–292.

Filippov, V. M. (2000). Istoricheskii shans na obnovlenie [Historic chance for renewal]. *Vestnik Vysshei Shkoly, 12,* 12–15.

Fink, I. (1997). Adapting facilities for new technologies and learners. In M.W. Peterson, D.D. Dill, and L.A. Mets (Eds.), *Planning and management for a changing environment* (pp. 319–339). San Francisco, CA: Jossey-Bass.

Friedland, R. & Alford, R. R. (1991). Bringing society back in: Symbols, practices, and institutional contradictions. In W. W. Powell & P. DiMaggio (Eds.), *The new institutionalism in organizational analysis* (pp. 232–263). Chicago, IL: The University of Chicago Press.

Fullan, M. (1991). *The new meaning of educational change.* New York: Teachers College Press.

Fusfeld, D. R. (1999). *The age of the economist.* Reading, MA: Addison-Wesley.

Gabriel, Y. (1998). The use of stories. In G. Symon & C. Cassell (Eds.), *Qualitative methods and analysis in organizational research* (pp. 135–160). Thousand Oaks, CA: Sage.

———. (2000). *Storytelling in organizations: Facts, fictions, and fantasies.* New York: Oxford University Press.

Garfinkel, H. (1967). *Studies in ethnomethodology.* Englewood Cliffs, NJ: Prentice-Hall.

Gaudillière, J.-P. & Löwy, I. (1998). *The invisible industrialist: Manufacturers and the production of scientific knowledge.* University of Manchester: Center for the History of Science, Technology, and Medicine.

Gerschenkron, A. (1978). Samuelson in Soviet Russia: A report. *Journal of Economic Literature, 16,* 560–573.

Gibson, K. (2003). Arguing artificially: A rhetorical analysis of the debates that have shaped cognitive science. *Business Communication Quarterly, 66* (2), 83–90.

Giddens, A. (1979). *Central problems in social theory.* Berkley, CA: University of California Press.

Gieryn, T. F. (1995). Boundaries of science. In S. Jasanoff, G.E. Markle, J.C. Petersen & T. Pinch (Eds.), *Handbook of science and technology studies* (pp. 393–444). Thousand Oaks, CA: Sage.

———. (1999). *Cultural boundaries of science: Credibility on the line.* Chicago, IL: The University of Chicago Press.

Globokar, T. (1997). Eastern Europe meets West: An empirical study on French management in a Slovenian plant. In S. A. Sackmann (Ed.), *Cultural complexity in organizations: Inherent contrasts and contradictions* (pp.72–86). Thousand Oaks, CA: Sage.

Goskomstat. (2002). *Handbook: Russia in figures.* Moscow: Goskomstat.

Graves, W. H., Henshaw, R. G., Oberlin, J. L. & Parker, A. S. (1997). Infusing information technology into the academic process. In M.W. Peterson, D.D. Dill, L.A. Mets (Eds.), *Planning and management for a changing environment* (pp. 432–452). San Francisco, CA: Jossey-Bass.

Gregory, J. & Miller, S. (1998). *Science in public: Communication, culture, and credibility.* New York and London: Plenum Trade.

Grunow, D. (1995). The research design in organization studies: Problems and prospects. *Organization Science, 6* (1), 93–103.

Guba, E.G. & Y. S. Lincoln. (2001). Competing paradigms in qualitative research. In C. F. Conrad, J. G. Haworth & L. R. Latucca (Eds.), *Qualitative research in higher education: ASHE reader series* (2nd edition) (pp. 57–72). Boston, MA: Pearson Custom Publishing.

Hage, J. & Aiken, M. (1970). *Social change in complex organizations.* New York: Random House.

Hahn, G. M. (2002). *Russia's revolution from above, 1985–2000: Reform transition, and revolution in the fall of the Soviet communist regime.* New Brunswick, N.J.: Transaction Publishers.

Hammond, M. F. (1984). Survival of small private colleges: Three case studies. *Journal of Higher Education, 55* (3), 369–388.

Haraway, D. J. (1997). Modest_Witness@Second_Millenium.FemaleMan©_Meets_OncoMouse™. New York: Routledge.

Harding, S. (1991). *Whose science? Whose knowledge?* Ithaca, NY: Cornell University Press.

Hartley, J. F. (1994). Case studies in organizational research. In C. Cassell & G. Symon (Eds.), *Qualitative methods in organizational research* (pp. 208–229). Thousand Oaks, CA: Sage.

Harvey, E. & Mills, R. (1970). Patterns of organizational adaptation: a political perspective. In M. N. Zald (Ed.), *Power in organizations.* Nashville: Vanderbilt University Press.

Hatim, B. & Mason, I. (1990). *Discourse and the translator.* London & New York: Longman.

Herman, D. (2002). *Story logic: Problems and possibilities of narratives.* Lincoln, NE: University of Nebraska Press.

Hickson, M, III. (2000). Relationships among central administrators, chairs, and faculty: Academic change agents in theory and practice. *Journal of the Association for Communication Administration, 29,* 273–85.

Higher School of Economics. (n.d.). *O V-SH-E.* [About HSE]. Retrieved July 02, 2004, from the Higher School of Economics site: http://www.hse.ru/rector_net/default.html

Huberman, A. M. & Miles, M. B. (1984). *Innovation up close: How school improvement works.* New York: Plenum Press.

Ivanov, M. A. & Magun, V. S. (2004). Issledovaniya kachestva vysshego ekonomichekogo obrazovaniya [Study of the quality of economic higher education]. *Ekonomicheskaya Shkola, 2.*

Journal of Economic Literature Classification System. (n.d.). Retrieved July 07, 2004, from *http://www.aeaweb.org/journal/jel_class_system.html*

Kachurovskaya, A. & Taratuta, Y. (2004). *Rektory idut v repetitory v ministru obrazovaniya i nauki* [Rectors become tutors of the Minister of Education and Science]. Retrieved July 02, 2004, from Moscow State University site: http://www.msu.ru/press/smiaboutmsu.html?2004–04–09_16–07.Obd9d6d

Keller, E. F. (1988). Feminist perspectives on science studies. *Science, Technology & Human Values, 13,* 235–249.

King, N. (1990). Innovation at work: The research literature. In M. West & J. L. Farr (Eds.), *Innovation and creativity at work: Psychological and organizational strategies,* (pp.15–61). New York: John Wiley & Sons.

Kitaev, I.V. (1994). Russian education in transition: Transformation of labor market, attitudes of youth and changes in management of higher and lifelong education. *Oxford Review of Education, 20,* 111–130.

Klyachko, T. L. (2001). Novyi organizatsionno-ekonomicheskii mehanism—reshaushchaya predposylka razvitia obrazovania [New organizational economic mechanism—a determinant premise of educational development]. *Vyssheye obrazovanie segodnya, 2,* 12–17.

Knorr-Cetina, K. (1992). The couch, the cathedral, and the laboratory: On the relationship between experiment and laboratory in science. In A. Pickering (Ed.), *Science as practice and culture* (pp. 65–113). Chicago, IL: The University of Chicago Press.

———. (1995). Laboratory studies: The cultural approach to the study of science. In S. Jasanoff, G.E. Markle, J.C. Petersen & T. Pinch (Eds.), *Handbook of science and technology studies* (pp. 140–167). Thousand Oaks, CA: Sage.

———. (1999). *Epistemic cultures: How the sciences make knowledge.* Cambridge, MA: Harvard University Press.

Kolesov, V. P. (2001). Ekonomicheskomu fakultetu 60 let [The Economic Faculty is 60 years old]. In V. P. Kolesov & V. P. Pankratova (Eds.), *Ekonomicheskii Fakultet 60 Let* (pp. 5–21). Moscow, Russia: Teis.

Komarov, S. (2002). *Garvardskiye shaluny* [Harvard jokers]. Retrieved July 02, 2004, from the Higher School of Economics site: http://www.hse.ru/pressa2002/default.php?show=6013@selected=9

Kovzik, A. & Watts, M. (2001). Reforming undergraduate instruction in Russia, Belarus, and Ukraine. *Journal of Economic Education, 32,* 78–92.

Kuzminov, Y. I. (2000, October 16). Tehnologia novogo ravenstva [Technology of new equality]. *Expert*. Retrieved July 02, 2004, from http://www.expert.ru/ expert/special/educat/kuzminov.htm

Kuzminov, Y. I., Klyachko, T.L., Belyakov, S.A., Drugov, M.A., Korolev, I.B., Skorovarova, N.A., Vassiliev, D.A., & Zaborovskaya, A.S. (2002). *Modernization of Russian education: Governmental Individual Financial Obligations*. Moscow: Higher School of Economics.

LaFollette, M. C. (1990). *Making science our own: Public Images of Science, 1910–1055*. Chicago, IL: Chicago University Press.

Latour, B. (1984). *The pasteurization of France*. Cambridge, MA: Harvard University Press.

———. (1986). The powers of association. In J. Law (Ed.), *Power, action and belief: A new sociology of knowledge?* (pp. 264–280). London, UK: Routledge & Kegan Paul.

———. (1987). *Science in action: How to follow scientists and engineers through society*. Cambrdige, MA: Harvard University Press.

———. (1996). *Aramis or the love of technology*. Cambridge, MA: Harvard University Press.

———. (1999). *Pandora's hope: Essays on the reality of science studies*. Cambridge, MA: Harvard University Press.

Latour, B. & Woolgar, S. (1979). *Laboratory life. The social construction of scientific facts*. London: Sage.

Lenoir, T. (1993). The discipline of nature and the nature of disciplines. In E. Messer-Davidow, D. R. Shumway, & D.J. Sylvan (Eds.), *Knowledges: Historical and critical studies in disciplinarity* (pp. 70–102). Charlottesville, VA: University Press of Virginia.

———. (1997). *Institutionalizing science: The cultural production of scientific disciplines*. Stanford, CA: Stanford University Press.

Lewis, D. R., Hendel, D. & Demyanchuk, A. (2003). *Private higher education in transition countries*. Kiev, Ukraine: KM Academia.

Lynch, M. (1985). *Art and artifact in laboratory science: A study of shop work and shop talk in a research laboratory*. London: Routledge & Kegan Paul.

Magun, A. V. (2003). *The concept and the experience of revolution: France 1789-/Russia 1985-* Unpublished doctoral dissertation, University of Michigan, U.S.A.

March, J. G. & Olsen, J. P. (1989). *Rediscovering institutions. The organizational basis of politics*. New York: Free Press.

Marshall, C. & Rossman, G. B. (1995). *Designing qualitative research* (2nd ed.), Thousand Oaks, CA: Sage.

Martinsons, M. G. & Valdemarsas, K. (1992). Technology and innovation mismanagement in the Soviet enterprise. *International Journal of Technology Management v. 7*, 359–69.

May, R., Young, C. B. & Ledgerwood, D. (1998). Lessons from Russian human resource management experience. *European Management Journal, 16*, 447–459.

McAuley, M. (1997). *Russia's politics of uncertainty*. New York, NY: Cambridge University Press.

McFaul, M. (2001). *Russia's unfinished revolution : Political change from Gorbachev to Putin.* Ithaca, N.Y. : Cornell University Press.

Merton, R. K. (1957). *Social theory and social structure.* New York: Free Press.

———. (1978). *The sociology of science: Theoretical and empirical investigations.* Chicago and London: The University of Chicago Press.

Meyer, J. W. (1992a). Centralization of funding and control in educational governance. In J. W. Meyer & W. R. Scott (Eds.), *Organizational environments: Ritual and rationality* (pp.179–198). Newberry Park, CA: Sage.

———. (1992b). Conclusion: Institutionalization and the rationality of formal organizational structure. In J. W. Meyer & W. R. Scott (Eds.), *Organizational environments: Ritual and rationality* (pp. 261–281). Newberry Park, CA: Sage.

———. (1992c). Innovation and knowledge use in American public education. In J. W. Meyer & W. R. Scott (Eds.), *Organizational environments: Ritual and rationality* (pp.233–260). Newberry Park, CA: Sage.

———. (1992d). Organizational factors affecting legalization in education. In J. W. Meyer & W. R. Scott (Eds.), *Organizational environments: Ritual and rationality* (pp.217–232). Newberry Park, CA: Sage.

———. (1977). The effects of education as an institution. *American Journal of Sociology, 83,* 55–77.

Meyer, J. W. & Rowan, B. (1991). Institutionalized organizations: Formal structure as myth and ceremony. In W. W. Powell & P. DiMaggio (Eds.), *The new institutionalism in organizational analysis* (pp. 41–63). Chicago, IL: The University of Chicago Press.

———. (1992). The structure of educational organizations. In J. W. Meyer & W. R. Scott (Eds.), *Organizational environments: Ritual and rationality* (pp.71–98). Newberry Park, CA: Sage.

Meyer, J. W., Scott, W. R. & Deal, T. R. (1981). Institutional and technical sources of organizational structure: Explaining the structure of educational organizations. In H. D. Stein (Ed.), *Organization and the human services* (pp. 151–178). Philadelphia, PA: Temple University Press.

Meyer, K. & Møller, I. B. (1998). Managing deep restructuring: Danish experiences in Eastern Germany. *European Management Journal, 16,* 411–421.

Meyer, M. and Zucker, L. (1989). *Permanently failing organizations.* Newbury Park, CA: Sage.

Mezhdunarodnyi Simpozium "Ekonomicheskaya teoria" [International Symposium "Economic Theory"]. (2004). Retrieved July 08, 2004, from Moscow State University Economic Faculty site: http://www.econ.msu.ru/ds.php3?id=339.

Miles, M. B. & Huberman, A. B. (1984). *Analyzing qualitative data: A source book for new methods.* Beverly Hills, CA: Sage.

———. (1994). *Qualitative data analysis: An expanded sourcebook* (2d ed.). Thousand Oaks, CA: Sage.

Morril, C., Yalda, C., Adelman, M., Musheno, M., & Bejarano, C. (2000). Telling tales in school: Youth culture and conflict narratives. *Law and Society Review, 34,* 521–565.

Mulkay, M. (1977). The sociology of scientific research community. In I. Spiegel-Rosing & D. de S. Price (Eds.), *Science, technology and society.* London: Sage.

Nakayama, S. (1984). *Academic and scientific traditions in China, Japan, and the West.* Tokyo, Japan: University of Tokyo Press.

Newman I. & Benz, C. R. (1998). *Qualitative-quantitative research methodology: Exploring the interactive continuum.* Carbondale, IL: Southern Illinois University Press.

Nikandrov, N. D. (1997). Issues and prospects for research on higher education in the Russian Federation. In J. Sadlak & P.G. Altbach (Eds.), *Higher education research at the turn of the new century: Structures, issues, and trends* (pp.251–269). New York: Garland.

Nord, W. R. & Tucker, S. (1987). *Implementing routine and radical innovations.* Lexington, MA: Lexington Books.

Nowotny, H., Scott, P., & Gibbons, M. (2001). *Re-thinking science: Knowledge and the public in an age of uncertainty.* Cambridge, UK: Polity.

Numagami, T. (1998). The infeasibility of invariant laws in management studies: A reflective dialogue in defense of case studies. *Organizational Science, 9* (1), 2–15.

Obloj, K. & Thomas, H. (1998). Transforming former state-owned companies into market competitors in Poland: The ABB experience. *European Management Journal, 16,* 390–399.

Obrazovatel'naya politika Rossii na sovremennom etape [Educational policy in Russia in the contemporary period]. (2002). *Vysshee obrazovanie v Rossii, 1,* 20–30.

OECD. (1998). *Review of National Policies for Education: Russian Federation.* Paris, France: OECD.

———. (1999). *Reviews of National Policies for Education: Tertiary education and research in the Russian Federation.* Paris, France: OECD.

Ofer, G. & Polterovich, V. (2000). Modern economics education in TEs: Technology transfer in Russia. *Comparative Economic Studies, 42* (2), 5–35.

Parsons, T. (1937). *The structure of social action.* New York: McGraw-Hill.

Perrow, C. (1986). *Complex organizations* (3rd Ed.). New York: Random House.

Peterson, M.W. (1997). Using contextual planning to transform institutions. In M.W. Peterson, D.D. Dill, & L.A. Mets (Eds.), *Planning and management for a changing environment* (pp. 127–157). San Francisco, CA: Jossey-Bass.

Peterson, M.W. & Dill, D. D. (1997). Understanding the competitive environment of the postsecondary knowledge industry. In M.W. Peterson, D.D. Dill, & L.A. Mets (Eds.), *Planning and management for a changing environment* (pp. 3–29). San Francisco, CA: Jossey-Bass.

Pickering, A. & Stephanides, A. (1992). Constructing quaternions: On the analysis of conceptual practice. In A. Pickering (Ed.), *Science as practice and culture* (pp. 113–139). Chicago, IL: The University of Chicago Press.

Pickering, A. (1995). *The mangle of practice: Time, agency, and science.* Chicago, IL: The University of Chicago Press.

Piskunov, D. (1996). Russia: higher education and change. In A. D. Tillett & B. Lesser (Eds.), *Science and technology in Central and Eastern Europe: The reform of higher education*. New York: Garland Publishing.

Pleskovic, B., Aslund, A., Bader, W. & Campbell, R. (2000). State of the art in economics education and research in transition economies. *Comparative Economic Studies*, 42 (2), 65–108.

Ranson, S., Hinings, B., and Greenwood, R. (1980). The structuring of organizational structures. *Administrative Science Quarterly*, Vol. 25, 1–17.

Ramirez, F. O. & Meyer, J. W. (1980). Comparative education: The social construction of the modern world system. *Annual Review of Sociology*, 6, 369–399.

Reznik, S. D. (2001a). Formirovaniye i razvitie upravlencheskogo personala vysshih uchebnih zavedenii. In A. T. Tertyshniy (Ed.), *Vysshee obrazovanie v Rossii: Dostizhenia i perspektivy* (pp. 76–78). Ekaterinburg, Russia: Izdatel'stvo Uralskogo Gosugarstvennogo Ekonomicheskogo Universiteta.

Reznik, S. D. (2001b). Sistema nepreryvnoi prakticheskoi podgotovki i trudoustroistva studentov vysshih uchebnih zavedenii [The system of continuous practical training and employment of students of higher education institutions]. In A. T. Tertyshniy (Ed.), *Vysshee obrazovanie v Rossii: Dostizhenia i perspektivy* (pp. 56–75). Ekaterinburg, Russia: Izdatel'stvo Uralskogo Gosugarstvennogo Ekonomicheskogo Universiteta.

Rhea, J. (1992, November-December). Prospecting for science in the former Soviet Union. *Research Technology Management*, 35, 13–17.

Roberts, J. S. (1999). A rhetorical analysis of the self in an organization: The production and reception of discourse in a bank. *Business Communication Quarterly*, 62 (2), 112–117.

Rogers, E. M. (1983). *Diffusion of innovations* (3rd ed.). New York: Free Press.

Rogers, E. M. & Shoemaker, F.F. (1971). *Communication of innovation: A cross-cultural approach*. New York: Free Press.

Rottenberg, R. (1996). When organization travels: On intercultural translation. In B. Czarniawska & G. Sevón (Eds.), *Translating organizational change* (pp. 191–240). Berlin and New York: Walter de Gruyter.

Rushing, F. W. (1994). The changing face of economics instruction in Russia. In W. B. Walstad (Ed.), *An international perspective on economic education* (pp. 231–254). Boston, MA: Kluwer Academic Publishers.

Rutland, P. (1999). Mission Impossible? The IMF and the failure of the market transition in Russia. *Review of International Studies* (25), 183–200.

Sadovnichii, V. (2000). Vysshaya shkola Rossii: orientiry na budushcheye [Russia's higher education: orientations for the future]. *Vestnik Vysshei Shkoly*, 12, 3–9.

Sahlin-Andersson, K. & Sevón, G. (2003). Imitation and identification as performatives. In B. Czarniawska & G. Sevón (Eds.), *The Northern Lights: Organization theory in Scandinavia* (pp. 249–267). Trelleborg, Sweden: Berlings Skogs.

Scott, W. R. (1998). *Organizations: Rational, natural and open systems* (4th ed.). Upper Saddle River, NJ: Prentice Hall.

Schiebinger, L. (1989). *The mind has no sex? Women in the origins of modern science*. Cambridge, MA: Harvard University Press.

Selznick, P. (1949). *TVA and the grass roots.* Berkley, CA: University of California Press.

Sevón, G. (1996). Organizational imitation in identity transformation. In B. Czarniawska & G. Sevón (Eds.), *Translating organizational change* (pp. 49–69). Berlin and New York: Walter de Gruyter.

Sevruk, M. A. (Ed.). (2002). *Federal'nye okruga i regiony* [Federal okrugs and regions]. In M. E. Sevruk (Ed.), Entsiklopedia Rossiya (p. 277). Moscow, Russia: Mezhdunarodnyi universitet "Sodruzhestvo."

Shaw, S. O., Burakova, N. & Makoukha, V. (2000). Economic education in Russia: A case study. *S.A.M. Advanced Management Journal,* 65 (3), 29–34.

Shutz, A. (1967). *The phenomenology of the social world.* Evanston, IL: Norwestern University Press.

Sokolin, V. L. (Ed.). (2002). *Rossiyskii statisticheskii ezhegodnik 2002.* [Russian annual statistical book 2002]. Moscow, Russia: Gosudarstvennii Komitet RF po statistike.

Sørensen, K. H. (1992). Towards a feminized technology? Gendered values in the construction of technology. *Social Studies of Science,* 22 (1), 5–31.

Stake, R. S. (1995). *The art of case study research.* Thousand Oaks, CA: Sage.

Stark, D. (2001). Ambiguous assets for uncertain environments: Heterarchy in post-socialist firms. In P. DiMaggio (Ed.), *The twenty-first century firm: Changing economic organization in international perspective* (pp. 68–104). Princeton, NJ: Princeton University Press.

Stark, J. & Letucca, L. (1997). *Shaping the college curriculum: Academic plans in action.* Boston and London: Allyn and Bacon.

Stensaker, B. & Norgard, J. D. (2001). Innovation and isomorphism: A case-study of university identity struggle 1969–1999. *Higher Education,* 42, 473–92.

Stuart, R. (2000). Introduction: Teaching modern economics in transition economics. *Comparative Economic Studies,* 42 (2),1–3.

Symon, G. & Cassell, C. (1998). Reflections on the use of qualitative methods. In G. Symon & C. Cassell (Eds.), *Qualitative methods and analysis in organizational research* (pp. 1–9). Thousand Oaks, CA: Sage.

Tashakkori, A. & Teddlie, C. (1998). Mixed methodology: Combining qualitative and quantitative approaches. *Applied Social Science Methods Series,* 46. Thousand Oaks, CA: Sage.

Tikhomirov, V. (2002). Otkrytoe obrazovanie v Rossii: ozhidania i pervye rezultaty [Open education in Russia: expectations and first results. *Vestnik?????? Vysshei Shkoly,* 5, 4–7.

Taylor, C. A. (1996). *Defining science: A rhetoric of demarcation.* Madison, WI: The University of Wisconsin Press.

Taylor, F. W. (1911). *The principles of scientific management.* New York: Harper.

Toumey, C. P. (1996). *Conjuring science: Scientific symbols and cultural meanings in American life.* New Brunswick, NJ: Rutgers University Press.

Tsoukas, H. (1989). The validity of ideographic research explanations. *Academy of Management Review,* 89, 551–563.

Van Loon, R. (2001). Organizational change: A case study. *Innovative Higher Education,* 25, 285–301.

Voogt, J. M. (1998). Functions and formats of curriculum standards: A comparison of standards in the Russian Federation, the Netherlands and England & Wales. In J. Voogt & T. Plomp (Eds.), *Education standards and assessment in the Russian Federation: Results from Russian-Dutch cooperation in education* (pp. 27–38). Leuven, Belgium: Acco.

Walstad, W.B. (2001). Improving Assessment in University Economics. *Journal of Economic Education, Vol. 32* (3), pp. 281–295.

Watson, T. J. (1995). Rhetoric, discourse and argument in organizational sense making: A reflexive tale. *Organization Studies, 16*, 805–822.

Weick, K.E. (1995). *Sensemaking in organizations.* Thousand Oaks, CA: Sage.

Westney, D. E. (1987). *Imitation and innovation: The transfer of Western Organizational patterns to Meiji Japan.* Cambridge, MA: Harvard University Press.

Westrum, R. (1990). Environments for innovation: Calculative and generative rationality in technology. In S. E. Cozzens & T. F. Gieryn (Eds.), *Theories of science in society* (pp.212–234). Bloomington, IN: Indiana University Press.

Williams, D. M. (2000). Representations of nature on the Mongolian steppe: An investigation of scientific knowledge production. *American Anthropologist, 102*, 503–519.

White book: The development of education in the Russian Federation. Part I. (2000). Moscow: MESI Publishing House.

Wolverton, M. (1998). Champions, agents, and collaborators: Leadership keys to successful systemic change. *Journal of Higher Education Policy and Management, 20* (1), 19–30.

Xin, K. R. & Pearce, J. L. (1996). Guanxi: Connections as substitutes for formal institutional support. *The Academy of Management Journal, 39*, 1641–1658.

Yin, R. K. (1989). *Case study research: Design and methods.* Thousand Oaks, CA: Sage.

Zaltman, G., Duncan, R. & Holbek, J. (1973). *Innovations and organizations.* New York: Wiley.

Zhelnorova, N. (1990, March 31–April 6). Est' li vyhod is krizisa? [Is there an exit from the crisis?]. *Argumenti i Fakti*, pp. 1, 2

Index

Printed in the United States
by Baker & Taylor Publisher Services